Neurogenetic Diagnoses

As world populations continue to age, the incidence of very common, ultimately fatal, neurodegenerative diseases (some of medicine's most puzzling illnesses) will increase exponentially. *Neurogenetic Diagnoses: The power of hope and the limits of today's medicine* explores the diverse impacts and intense meanings of genetic diagnoses for patients suffering from such diseases, and for their family caregivers and clinicians. Through richly-textured, often heart-wrenching longitudinal case studies, *Neurogenetic Diagnoses* reveals how extremely difficult it can be for patients to obtain a definitive diagnosis for the cause of their symptoms, even with genetic testing; how, with or without definitive diagnoses, patients and family care-givers strive to come to terms with their situations; and how they are aided (or not) in these endeavors by their doctors. The analysis is framed by increasingly sharp social debate over the consequences of decoding the human genome – and the impact of genetic technology on our lives.

Carole H. Browner is Professor in the Department of Anthropology, the Department of Women's Studies, and the Center for Culture and Health, which is based at UCLA's David Geffen School of Medicine NPI-Semel Institute for Neuroscience and Human Behavior, USA. She is also editor of the collection. *Reproduction, Globalization and the State: New Theoretical and Ethnographic Perspectives* (Duke University Press, 2010).

H. Mabel Preloran has over 25 years experience as a cultural anthropologist in the USA and in Latin America. She is a Research Anthropologist in UCLA's David Geffen School of Medicine NPI-Semel Institute for Neuroscience and Human Behavior, USA. Her current research focuses on the use of genetic testing in neurology.

Genetics and Society

Series Editors:

Paul Atkinson, *Distinguished Research Professor in Sociology, Cardiff University*,

Ruth Chadwick, *Director of Cesagen, Cardiff University*,

Peter Glasner, *Professorial Research Fellow for Cesagen, Cardiff University*,

Brian Wynn, *Associate Director of Cesagen, Lancaster University*

The books in this series, all based on original research, explore the social, economic and ethical consequences of the new genetic sciences. The series is based in the ESRC's Centre for Economic and Social Aspects of Genomics (Cesagen), the largest UK investment in social-science research on the implications of these innovations. With a mix of research monographs, edited collections, textbooks and a major new handbook, the series will be a major contribution to the social analysis of new agricultural and biomedical technologies.

Series titles include:

Governing the Transatlantic Conflict over Agricultural Biotechnology
Contending coalitions, trade liberalisation and standard setting
Joseph Murphy and Les Levidow

New Genetics, New Social Formations
Peter Glasner, Paul Atkinson and Helen Greenslade

New Genetics, New Identities
Paul Atkinson, Peter Glasner and Helen Greenslade

The GM Debate
Risk, politics and public engagement
*Tom Horlick-Jones, John Walls, Gene Rowe, Nick Pidgeon,
Wouter Poortinga, Graham Murdock and Tim O'Riordan*

Growth Cultures
Life sciences and economic development
Philip Cooke

Human Cloning in the Media
Joan Haran, Jenny Kitzinger, Maureen McNeil and Kate O'Riordan

Local Cells, Global Science
Embryonic stem cell research in India
Aditya Bharadwaj and Peter Glasner

Handbook of Genetics and Society
Paul Atkinson, Peter Glasner and Margaret Lock

The Human Genome
Chamundeeswari Kuppuswamy

Debating Human Genetics
Contemporary issues in public policy and ethics
Alexandra Plows

Community Genetics and Genetic Alliances
Eugenics, carrier testing, and networks of risk
Aviad Raz

Genetic Testing
Accounts of autonomy, responsibility and blame
Michael Arribas-Ayllon, Srikant Sarangi and Angus Clarke

GM Food on Trial
Testing European democracy
Les Levidow and Susan Carr

Scientific, Clinical and Commercial Development of the Stem Cell
From radiobiology to regenerative medicine
Alison Kraft

The Making of a Syndrome
The case of Rett Syndrome
Katie Featherstone and Paul Atkinson

Barcoding Nature
Claire Waterton, Rebecca Ellis and Brian Wynne

Gender and Genetics
Towards a sociological account of prenatal screening
Kate Reed

Neurogenetic Diagnoses
The power of hope and the limits of today's medicine
Carole H. Browner and H. Mabel Preloran

Neurogenetic Diagnoses

The power of hope and the limits of today's medicine

**Carole H. Browner and
H. Mabel Preloran**

Routledge
Taylor & Francis Group

LONDON AND NEW YORK

First published 2010
by Routledge
2 Park Square, Milton Park, Abingdon, Oxon, OX14 4RN

Simultaneously published in the USA and Canada
by Routledge
270 Madison Ave, New York NY 10016

Routledge is an imprint of the Taylor & Francis Group, an informa business

Transferred to Digital Printing 2010

Typeset in Times New Roman by Swales & Willis Ltd, Exeter, Devon

British Library Cataloguing in Publication Data
A catalogue record for this book is available
from the British Library

Library of Congress Cataloging-in-Publication Data
Browner, C. H. (Carole H.), 1947–
    Neurogenetic diagnoses: the power of hope, and the limits of today's
    medicine / Carole H. Browner and H. Mabel Preloran.
    p. cm.—(Genetic and society)
    Includes bibliographical references.
    1. Nervous system—Diseases—Diagnosis. 2. Neurogenetics.
    I. Preloran, H. Mabel. II. Title.
    RC348.B835 2009
    616.8'0442—dc22
    2009027149

ISBN10: 0–415–56365–8 (hbk)
ISBN10: 0–415–59256–9 (pbk)
ISBN10: 0–203–86340–2 (ebk)

ISBN13: 978–0–415–56365–9 (hbk)
ISBN13: 978–0–415–59256–7 (pbk)
ISBN13: 978–0–203–86340–4 (ebk)

En memoria de Jorge—and for Richard

Contents

Foreword

The practice of medicine is being fundamentally transformed by genetics. Some have referred to this as a "genetic revolution," but it has actually (and appropriately) been an evolution. One could say that it began in the nineteenth century with the ingenious discoveries of Darwin and Mendel, which were much later applied to the astute clinical observations of physicians such as Friedreich, Huntington, and Charcot. A more precise beginning might be the discovery of the DNA double helix by Watson and Crick in 1953 followed a few years later by the first medical genetics clinics in the United States started by Moltulsky, McKusick, and Neel. However, even these critical events did not really energize the practice of medicine. The fundamental change truly began in the 1990s with the discovery of genes causing specific human diseases. These events merged with the successful human genome project to produce an avalanche of information leading to a far better understanding of the molecular basis of human biology and pathology. An important byproduct of this new information has been the advent of genetic testing.

It has been intriguing to notice how much of early gene discovery and genetic testing has been related to diseases of the nervous system. This was not a coincidence and occurred for at least two reasons. First, the disabilities produced by neurologic disorders frequently cannot be "hidden" and conditions such as weakness, abnormal movements, and dementia are often all too obvious. Second, many neurologic diseases have traditionally been considered "classics" of human genetics such as Huntington's disease, Friedreich's ataxia, neurofibromatosis and Duchenne, and myotonic muscular dystrophies. These diseases have fascinated and puzzled physicians and geneticists for generations. It is not surprising that they play a prominent role in discussions of genetic testing.

Genetic testing for human diseases falls into two overlapping but fairly distinct categories. First, a doctor may do a genetic test on a person with signs and symptoms of a disease in order to prove or exclude a specific diagnosis. The genetic tests are often considered the gold standard of diagnosis. This is called diagnostic genetic testing. Second, genetic tests may be obtained on family members who have absolutely no symptoms or signs of the disease in their family, but wish to know if they have inherited the abnormal gene. This is called pre-symptomatic or asymptomatic genetic testing. Both types of testing are fraught with subtleties and complexities that are often not apparent to the patient, their family members, or their physicians. In this book Browner and Preloran focus on the subtleties and complexities of diagnostic testing for neurogenetic diseases. This is not a book about molecular biology, or genetic technology, or the genetic testing marketplace, or the role of genetic testing in differential diagnosis. Rather, it is a detailed and often poignant exploration of the impact of genetic testing on individuals and their families. There is a brief overview describing why some people choose or do not choose to proceed with genetic testing. However, the bulk of the book is a careful dissection of the role of genetic testing in the lives of four very different patients. There are several insightful interviews with their neurology physicians, but the emphasis is on how patients and their families deal (or fail to deal) with the fall-out of genetic testing.

We discover from this book that the world of genetic testing swirls with confusion, disagreement, depression, dissatisfaction, and suspicion. On the other hand, testing may also result in useful knowledge, clarification, resolution, new perspectives, new relationships, and life altering changes. It becomes clear that genetic testing touches some of the most intimate and personal aspects of patients' lives including marriage, child bearing, parenting, career choices, finances, travel, and every kind of relationship. To successfully navigate these genetic testing waters requires knowledge, wisdom, experience, compassion, patience, and caution. Meeting these requirements is a difficult challenge and these attributes are often in short supply.

As a practicing neurogeneticist I can confirm that the stories related in this book accurately reflect the real world of genetic testing. Although it is true that patients may struggle mightily with the results of genetic testing, it is also true that there are many remarkably courageous individuals who show a surprisingly flexible strength that allows them to cope with discouraging news. I can also attest to the need for professional genetic counselors. Their absence is noticeable in many of the scenarios described in this book. Genetic counselors bring an important expertise, knowledge, and perspective that will be increasingly needed in the new world of genetic medicine.

Browner and Preloran have done a magnificent job taking a potentially dry epidemiological study and turning it into a highly personal, but still scholarly exposition on the use of genetic testing. Who should read this book? It will benefit any patient, family, physician, or healthcare provider faced with a genetic disease. Since every family (yours and mine included) has a genetic disease lurking somewhere in the background, this will be a very wide audience indeed.

Thomas D. Bird, MD
Department of Neurology
University of Washington
VA Puget Sound Healthcare System
Seattle, WA

Preface

Neurogenetic Diagnoses: The power of hope and the limits of today's medicine examines the complex and challenging experiences of patients suffering from degenerative neurological diseases for which no cures presently exist. These diseases are extremely common and, as populations age, are increasing exponentially in the U.S. and elsewhere. We focus on newly available genetic tests used to help diagnose these patients' conditions, and their meaning and efficacy for patients, relatives, and clinicians. Through richly textured longitudinal case studies, this monograph reveals how very difficult it is for patients to discover the cause of their symptoms, even with genetic testing; how, with or without definitive test-based diagnoses, patients and their caregivers seek to come to terms with their situations; and how they are aided (or not) by their doctors in dealing with their afflictions. The research is framed by increasingly broad media attention to new advances in genetic science and medicine, and the associated acceleration of public interest in the relevance and ethicality of genetic testing.

While this work principally endeavors to provide students, researchers, and clinicians greater understanding and appreciation of the context and consequences of genetic testing for patients suffering neurodegenerative movement disorder symptoms, we hope it will also serve to enlighten and empower patients and their caregivers to better cope with the entire process – and to persevere, whatever diagnoses may ensue. (To this end, patients and caregivers should not hesitate to skip our academically oriented Introduction and proceed directly to Part I.)

Acknowledgments

The success of a large project like this inevitably owes an enormous debt to many individuals and institutions. We wish to thank the Ethical, Legal, and Social Issues (ELSI) Research Program of the National Institute for Human Genome Research for major funding through a grant on the "Use of Genetics in Neurologists' Clinical Practices," and Elizabeth J. Thomson, Program Officer, for her faith in this project since its inception and her longstanding support of our larger research agenda.

We also wish to thank the Semel Institute for Neuroscience and Human Behavior and its Center for Culture and Health, along with Professors Peter Whybrow, Fawzy L. Fawzy, Robert B. Edgerton, Thomas S. Weisner, M. Belinda Tucker, and Andrew J. Fuligni for providing a stimulating and supportive environment in which to advance the ideas developed here, and Warren Thomson, Gayle Hifumi Gaw, Marlo Duran, and Dario N. Mellado for outstanding administrative support. Maria Cristina Casado, Jennifer McGee, Jenny Musto, and Marissa Strickland provided expert research assistance, and Marissa Strickland also helped ready the manuscript for publication. Eli Lieber, Pascale Hess, Adriana Preloran, and Silvia Balzano offered keen insight at various stages of the research. Dora Trail warrants special thanks for diverse help and good-natured support, including introducing us to some of the clinicians, translating some of the tape transcripts from Spanish, and offering helpful comments on early chapter drafts. Jill Shapira first got us interested in the topic of genetics in neurology; Rayna Rapp and Barbara F. Crandall sagely put us on the path to investigating the social consequences of decoding the human genome. Richard Rosenthal helped immeasurably in sharpening our arguments and smoothing our prose. Just as we were going to press, Alice Wexler took the time to read the entire manuscript, raised excellent questions, and offered astute and exceptionally constructive suggestions.

Some of the material contained in these chapters was presented at the following venues: at the 2006 Annual Meeting of the American Anthropological Association in a symposium on "Temporality, Suffering, and Experience" organized by Jill Mitchell and Jason Throop; in a workshop coordinated by Marcelo Britos concerning "The Impact of Institutionalized Medical Services on Patients' Health" and one hosted by Marta Martinez on "Analyzing Research Instruments for Data-Gathering in Medical Settings," both at the National University of Tucuman, Argentina in 2006; in 2007, in a panel put together by Mara Buchbinder and Ignasci Clementi on

"Families in Pain: Illness, Suffering, and (Inter)subjectivity" held at the Biennial Meeting of the Society for Psychological Anthropology, at a workshop organized by Angel Aimeta at the Universidad Nacional de la Pampa in Santa Rosa, Argentina about "Medical Anthropology: Past, Present, and Future," and in a panel hosted by Clare Stacey on "Is a Caring Society Possible? Mobilizing for Change at The Fifth Carework Conference at the CUNY Graduate Center in New York City"; in a symposium on the impact of genetic testing on families at the "Translating 'ELSI': The Ethical, Legal, and Social Implications of Genomics" Conference held at Case Western Reserve University in Cleveland, Ohio in 2008; and in a symposium organized by Bill McKellin and Sylvie Fortin on "Creating and Crossing Medical Fields of Practice" at the 2009 Joint Annual Meetings of the Canadian Association of Social and Cultural Anthropology and the American Ethnological Association in Vancouver, BC.

Above all, our thanks go to the clinicians, patients, and families who trusted in us enough to participate in this research; some did so with genuine enthusiasm over the course of several years. For reasons of confidentiality, they must remain nameless. We offer them this volume with the hope that it will serve as a small token of our appreciation for the openness, generosity, and patience with which they shared the stories of their lives, their views on wide ranging subjects, and their experiences.

Introduction

It's hard to determine what's hype and what's not in the burgeoning field of human genetic science. The media breathlessly reports new developments almost daily, touting advances that purport to reveal nature's deepest secrets, like which gene makes grandpa a confirmed drinker, and why sister is so exceptionally mean. New research even claims that our food likes and dislikes are stored in our genes (Severson 2007). A simple cheek swab genetic test that purports to predict whether your child will excel at endurance sports like distance running, speed and power sports such as football, or a combination of both, is being marketed for just $149 (Macur 2008), and the director of the United States National Institute on Drug Abuse appears on a popular national television program admonishing that women with a certain genetic variant who smoke during pregnancy put their children at risk for future aggressive behavior problems (Volkow 2009). Throughout the post-industrial world, researching one's own family tree has grown so popular that one observer characterized the current era as "the age of household genetics" (Seabrook 2001). Still, as important a landmark as deciphering the human genetic code might someday prove to be, for now its practical uses reside principally in the area of medicine.

Indeed, dramatic advances in the past two decades have ushered in what is coming to be known as "the post-genome era"[1] of science and medicine (Oksenberg 2006). This has been accompanied by a growing expectation that genetic assessments intended to maximize medical care standards and patients' quality of life will soon become integral to routine healthcare (Guttmacher and Collins 2002; Varmus 2002). At the same time, a growing market in "direct-to-consumer" (DTC) genetic tests, which do not require a physician's prescription, also seems to be flourishing, although there is yet no evidence of any real health benefits from their use. The rising popularity of genetic testing notwithstanding, insufficient empirical attention has been devoted to examining the processes and consequences of the incorporation of genetic assessments into routine medical care (Bohnam and Terry 2008). Research has shown that the increasingly widespread use of genetic assessments in such specialized areas of medical care as prenatal diagnosis, cancer screening, and predictive testing of individuals at risk for autosomal dominant conditions has evoked a host of psychological, social, cultural, and bioethical issues (e.g. psychological distress, disclosure of familial risk, fears of stigma, occupational, and financial discrimination) (Alper *et al*. 2002; Broadstock, Michie, and Marteau 2000; Featherstone *et al*. 2005; Hallowell *et al*. 2003; Marteau and Richards 1999; Meiser *et al*. 2005; Rapp 2000), as well as broader socio-ethical dilemmas (Davis 2001; Knoppers and Chadwick 2005; Rothstein 1997). Moreover, results from an individual patient's genetic tests may have a direct impact on parents, siblings, and children, who may not have chosen to avail themselves of this information.

Neurology is a uniquely rich and exciting area in which to explore the impact of recent advances in medical genetics and genetic testing. It is estimated that 50 percent of the approximately 20,000 genes identified as making up the human genome are expressed in the brain and neurological system (Blasko 2006), and efforts to understand the actual roles of these genes have triggered an explosion of activity. Genetic tests to diagnose specific neurological conditions including hereditary ataxias, muscular dystrophies, hereditary neuropathies, torsion dystonia, and Huntington's disease are now commercially available (Gasser *et al*. 2003). These tests can be used to confirm a diagnosis in individuals with suggestive symptoms, and to a limited extent, may help predict the course of a patient's disease.

In addition, genetic components in a growing number of neurological conditions, including repeat expansion diseases, autism, and common diseases such as Parkinson's, stroke, epilepsy, and dementias are increasingly being identified and better understood (Bertram *et al*. 2000; Bird 1999; Eng-King and Jankovic 2006). Understanding, however, remains far from complete: some of the most common neurological conditions including Parkinson's and Alzheimer's appear not to be caused by single genes – but rather by complex multi-factorial traits that appear to involve genes modifying other genes and/or being influenced by environmental factors (Robinson, Fernald, and Clayton 2008). Furthermore, some gene alterations in and of themselves appear not to cause disease, but, rather, may alter a person's susceptibility or be involved in a disease mechanism (Blasko 2006). Therefore, while the most common neurological diseases appear to be the result of very complex interactions among many genes, epigenetic mechanisms (i.e. changes in gene expression caused by mechanisms other than changes in the underlying DNA sequence), and environmental factors, exactly how these factors interact to produce disease remains poorly understood (Hoop *et al*. 2006). Recent efforts to cast light on this subject through genome-wide association studies, which compare the genomes of patients with common diseases like cancer and diabetes to healthy people, in the hope of pinpointing the DNA changes responsible for them, are yielding disappointing results. In the few cases where shared DNA variants have been found, they appear to carry only a small risk for the disease in question (Goldstein 2009; Hardy and Singleton 2009).

Moreover, because neurological diseases are, at this time, incurable, many wonder about the very value of genetic testing beyond, in some cases, reproductive planning. Clinical medicine's core ethical precept, the so-called Hippocratic injunction to "above all, do no harm" has guided Western medicine's underlying values and objectives for treatment and cure for thousands of years (Sharpe and

Carter 2006a: 1). Today, the movement of genetics into mainstream medicine has evoked wide-ranging societal debates as to the nature of an appropriate model of care, given medicine's inability to cure or even effectively treat most genetic conditions (Callanan and LeRoy 2006).

Yet despite our growing understanding of the complex roles that genetic and genomic processes play in the manifestation of a wide range of neurological disorders, there have been neither large-scale surveys nor many in-depth analyses of what these scientific advances might mean to neurologists, neurology patients, their family caregivers, or neurology practice. This contrasts with other fields of medicine, in particular, psychiatry, family practice, internal medicine, and obstetrics and gynecology, which have seen significant empirical research on these subjects (Burke *et al.* 2002; Cunningham-Burley 2008; Emery *et al.* 1999; Freedman *et al.* 2003; Hoop *et al.* 2008; Pinsky *et al.* 2001). These studies find that clinicians and patients hold generally positive views about the value of genetic testing, given appropriate ethical and legal safeguards. This research has generated valuable material for understanding clinicians' attitudes, beliefs, and values. Still lacking, however (not just in neurology, but in other fields of medicine), are detailed empirical data about actual clinical practices. Because virtually nothing is known about what is taking place in doctors' offices when the subjects of genetics and genetic testing are raised, or the long-term consequences of these conversations for patients and caregivers, we set out to examine the meaning and use of information derived from genetic testing for neurology patients who were seeking a diagnosis, their families, and their clinicians.

Genetic testing in neurology

Although the idea of a human genetic "map" was first raised in the 1930s, it was not until the 1970s and 1980s that scientists had sufficiently developed the technologies and methods to actually isolate single human genes and identify their function. A gene is a sequence of nucleotides, or subunits of DNA or RNA, located at a specific spot on a chromosome that has been found to be associated with a particular trait and its variants. Each of our genes encodes a specific functional product, usually a protein. The order in which the nucleotides appear in the gene may vary slightly from one individual to the next, and this contributes to the variations in the trait as it is observed in a population. Known as alleles, these different variants of genes produce the mutations that cause a disease (Cunningham-Burley and Boulton 2000:176–77).

Advances in genetic science throughout the latter half of the twentieth century had led to the development of clinical tests for genes in individuals; these tests are known gene tests (also known as DNA-based tests). Such tests involve the examination of the sequence of nucleotides in an individual gene to identify anomalies in chromosomes, genes, or proteins. By analyzing the sequence of nucleotides in one or more particular genes, genetic tests can help explain or predict the development of certain clinical disorders. Today there are eight types of genetic tests available:

- **Pre-implantation genetic diagnosis (PGD)** is used to detect genetic anomalies in embryos that were created with assisted reproductive techniques such as in-vitro fertilization.
- **Prenatal testing** is performed during pregnancy to detect anomalies in a fetus's genes or chromosomes prior to birth.
- **Newborn screening** is employed just after birth to identify genetic disorders that can be treated early in life.
- **Carrier testing** identifies individuals who carry one copy of a gene mutation that, when present in two copies, causes a genetic disorder.
- **Predictive** or **pre-symptomatic testing** is used to detect gene mutations that increase a person's risk for developing disorders with a genetic basis.
- **Diagnostic testing** is employed to confirm or rule out a diagnosis when a particular genetic or chromosomal condition is suspected based on physical signs and symptoms.
- **Forensic testing** uses DNA sequences to identify an individual for legal purposes.
- **Direct-to-consumer (DTC) genetic testing** can be ordered directly from a number of companies without having to go through a healthcare professional. These tests typically do not identify causative mutations, but instead provide information about genetic variations that may potentially alter an individual's risk of a certain disease, the precise degree of which is generally uncertain or un-quantified.

At present, the most meaningful types of genetic testing in neurology are predictive/pre-symptomatic testing and diagnostic testing. In considering the benefits and burdens of genetic testing in neurology, Thomas D. B. Bird has observed:

> DNA testing for mutations in genes causing neurogenetic disorders is becoming a common practice in clinical neurology. The tests . . . are especially valuable in establishing diagnoses in symptomatic patients. These DNA tests are also used in asymptomatic persons at risk for genetic diseases who wish to determine whether or not they have inherited an abnormal gene. A number of complex issues need to be considered including precipitation of depression, prenatal diagnosis and testing of children, impact on insurance and employment, legal aspects, possible third-party coercion, and an understanding of each test's limitations. Therefore, these DNA tests need to be used with careful clinical judgment and in the context of each individual patient and family.
>
> (Bird 1999: 253).

Bird regards the use of diagnostic genetic testing for neurology patients who already have symptoms of what might prove to be a genetic disease as a straightforward procedure comparable to any other type of diagnostic testing. Two examples of the use of genetic testing for diagnostic purposes in neurology are to inform a patient with chorea that a blood test is positive for the gene for Huntington's disease, and to test a patient with muscle weakness to determine whether he or she carries a gene for myotonic dystrophy.

But Bird also recognizes that a primary difference between diagnostic genetic testing and any other type of diagnostic testing is that a genetic diagnosis can have genetic implications for other family members, and may potentially provoke questions and concerns (Bird 1999: 253), including fears of stigma, discrimination, risk of suicide, and other adverse psychological consequences. But it is also the case that being able to offer a patient a specific genetic diagnosis for their neurological symptoms may remove ambiguity and clarify their prognosis. In addition, a negative genetic test may encourage clinicians to continue to search for other causes of a patient's symptoms, although in some cases, administering the wrong genetic test may cause a clinician to miss other genetic causes of a disease. Another unfortunate complexity associated with the use of genetic testing to diagnose patients with neurological symptoms is that a patient with a disease-causing mutation may have symptoms mimicking the disease that are in fact caused by something other than the mutation (Bird 1999: 254).

Other unique features associated with both predictive and diagnostic genetic testing – in neurology and as well as in other fields of medicine – have raised alarm among many bioethicists and social observers. Some perceive a moral dilemma in identifying genetic causes for conditions that as yet have no cure (Burgess, Laberge, and Knoppers 1998; Edwards *et al.* 2008; Hoop *et al.* 2006; Paulson 2002). Information derived from genetic testing may also be perceived differently by patients and family members than from other diagnostic findings, with more far-ranging social implications (Davison, Macintyre, and Smith 1994; Emery 2001; Norrgard 2008). For example, it is almost inevitable that when a genetic diagnosis is given to an individual patient, the perception by other family members of their own personal risk status will elevate (Featherstone *et al.* 2005; Meiser and Dunn 2000; Quaid 1994). This issue takes on particular meaning in neurology clinical settings in which movement disorder patients go in search of medical attention. Many such patients depend on family caregivers not only to take them to medical visits, but also to play a critical role in decisions regarding the patient's medical care. Yet patients and family members may differ sharply in their interest and receptivity to genetic information, particularly if the family caregiver is a biological relative (Emery 2001; Finkler 2005; Peters, Djurdjinovic, and Baker 1999). The extent to which neurologists are aware of these special considerations when offering genetic testing to their patients introduces a host of new and challenging concerns.

For this reason, we set out to study factors that shape the views of patients suffering neurodegenerative movement disorder symptoms about genetics and genetic testing, and how they, their relatives, and their clinicians understand and use genetic information in the patients' medical care. Movement disorder symptoms are caused by a group of central nervous system diseases that impose progressive loss of strength, muscle mass, and mechanical range of motion. Those afflicted may experience slowed or limited movement, difficulties initiating movement, and additional or exaggerated movements (Aminoff, Greenberg, and Simon

2005). Our research focused on patients suffering from movement disorders that, in some cases, are known to have a genetic component, including Huntington's disease, essential tremor, and multiple forms of ataxia.[2]

There have been few, if any, general population surveys on the impact of advances in genetic knowledge on the lives of ordinary people. Work broadly related to the subject has more often looked at public attitudes associated with science policy rather than knowledge about genetics or the experiences of individuals actually afflicted with genetic diseases (Durant, Hansen, and Bauer 1996; Featherstone *et al.* 2005; Lanie *et al.* 2004; Wexler 1996). While there is a significant and growing literature on lay concepts of genetics, the populations recruited for these studies have typically been individuals or families seeking genetic counseling or who, for some other reason, have a special interest in the subject, such as a known family history of a genetic condition (e.g. Davison 1997; Finkler 2000; Gessen 2008; Heath 1998; Parsons and Atkinson 1992; Richards 1997).

Ongoing advances in genetic knowledge have increased speculation as to how individuals, families, and clinicians might or might not make use of genetic information, as well as about how such genetic knowledge might alter basic cultural values and understandings. Among the questions of interest in this regard are whether, and if so how, the science of genetics may be transforming sociality through the formation of new kinds of social groups and/or novel identities and identity practices that derive from a specific diagnosis or a disease (Gibbon and Novas 2008a; Schaffer, Kuczynski, and Skinner 2008; Taussig, Rapp, and Heath 2003). This monograph is, then, intended as a contribution to the vibrant and growing literature on these subjects and, more broadly, on the social impact of genetic technologies (see, for example, Becker 2000; Conrad and Gabe 2000; Edwards *et al.* 1999; Featherstone *et al.* 2005; Franklin 1997, 2007; Franklin, Lury, and Stacey 2000; Gibbon and Novas 2008b; Green *et al.* 2004; Konrad 2005; Lock, Young, and Cambrosio 2000; Novas and Rose 2000; Ong and Collier 2005; Rapp 2000; Rose 2007; Rothman 1986; Strathern 1992; Taussig 2009).

In the chapters that follow, we will examine the meaning and use of genetics and genetic diagnoses for patients suffering from neurodegenerative movement disorder symptoms, their family caregivers, and their clinicians. Our analyses will be contextualized and framed by patients' and caregivers' broader experiences living with neurodegenerative disease, the difficulties faced by clinicians in treating these disorders, and contexts in which the doctors regard genetic diagnoses as meaningful.

We will show that, in and of itself, a genetic diagnosis had no inherent or unitary meaning for those affected by neurodegenerative disease. Rather, the diagnosis was imbued with significance by a patient's or family caregiver's broader life histories and contemporary experiences. For some, a genetic diagnosis had exceptional meaning that transformed or reinforced their concepts of self and identity, family dynamics and interrelations, and their views about free will and predestination. For others, however, its meaning was much more concrete in that a positive genetic test provided a specific diagnosis that reduced their uncertainty, increased their feelings of control, and in a general sense, provided information that enabled them to better plan for – or imagine – what their future held in store. In this regard, the genetic diagnosis was like any other, except to the extent that the main burden was in knowing with certainty that their disease was incurable.

We similarly found that the relevance of genetic testing for the clinicians in our study was quite variable, and proved to be a function of a number of dimensions, including their training, experience, and the nature of their medical practice and patient populations. We therefore also consider whether and when genetic testing for neurodegenerative conditions appeared to help these clinicians better serve their patients and family caregivers – as well as to reduce their own anxieties in treating patients suffering from these incurable, ultimately fatal conditions.

Studying the impact of neurodegenerative disorders on patients and their families challenged us, as it did them, to look constantly to the past – as well as the future. Uniformly, patients asked the questions that all sick people inevitably ask: How will their disease change their lives and their sense of personal identity and wellbeing? What new issues might they have to face as they strive to integrate their illness into their present and anticipated future life situations? In the context of these broad but momentous questions, we focused first and foremost on the impact and meaning of a genetic diagnosis for a group of patients, family caregivers, and clinicians.

Who we are and how we came to be asking these research questions

We are anthropologists who, for the past 20 years, have been investigating the social impact of decoding the human genome, particularly with regard to how information derived from genetics shapes different aspects of health-related behavior. Our earliest work concerned fetal diagnosis, the area of medicine where the use of genetic testing has the longest history and is most routinized. Over the years, we conducted studies on the factors pregnant women (and in some cases, their male partners) of varying social class and ethnic background took into account when deciding whether to undergo prenatal diagnostic testing. These tests, the most widely used of which are blood screening, ultrasound, and amniocentesis, can detect many of the most common birth anomalies including chromosomal abnormalities like Down syndrome, developmental disabilities, and types of neural tube defects.

Our previous studies focused on the extent to which pregnant women and their partners actually wanted the information provided by fetal diagnosis, whether they were acquiescing to a perceived "technological imperative," or simply trying to please their clinicians (Browner and Press 1995; Browner and Preloran 2000a; Browner, Preloran, and Cox 1999). In fact, we found that healthcare providers' own attitudes about fetal diagnosis were the best predictors of whether the women opted for prenatal diagnosis (Browner and Preloran 2000b). To our great surprise, we found that interaction with physicians, nurses, and genetic counselors however, were not necessarily the most influential factors in that a significant proportion of the pregnant women, particularly recent immigrants, based their amniocentesis decisions not on those interactions, but on the recommendations of their clinic's clerks and receptionists who functioned in the role of *ad hoc* medical interpreters (Preloran, Browner, and Lieber 2005). Even more intriguing was the fact that even many women who said they were adamantly opposed to abortion did not feel free to turn down the tests – which, in the case of amniocentesis, has its own inherent risks including miscarriage. We also found that the practice of universally offering fetal diagnosis to all pregnant women raises additional problematic bioethical issues in that at present, as with all genetic testing, virtually none of the conditions detected have any effective treatment or cure.

In 2003, we shifted focus from the beginnings of life to its end – to investigate the experiences of adult patients with terminal neurodegenerative diseases. Doing so also involved a shift from a clinical setting where the meaning and use of genetic information was already highly institutionalized, and therefore expected, to one where it was just taking hold. We picked neurogenetics, in part, for this reason, and set out to investigate the processes and consequences of incorporating genetic testing into routine diagnosis and management procedures. By way of introduction to this project and the intellectual issues that surround it, we will begin by describing the basic assumptions we brought to this investigation: assumptions based on our own earlier work, the social scientific literature, and our own general knowledge of the subject.

Given that we were studying genetic conditions, we had expected that *stigma* would be an important element of concern; this is a major theme in the literature on the social and psychological concomitants of genetic disorders (Sharpe and Carter 2006b). Instead, much more often, we found that the "flip side" of stigma – the legitimatizing effect of actually, and in many cases, finally, having a diagnosis, and the reduction of uncertainty that comes from having *any* diagnosis – was far more meaningful to the patients and their families; any special sense of burden associated with the knowledge that the problem was caused by a genetic defect generally paled in significance. This is because many had been suffering from progressively worsening symptoms that had resisted diagnosis, some since childhood, even as they visited doctor after doctor in vain quest for an explanation. Finally finding their experience clinically validated freed these patients from the agonizing stigma they had long endured: being labeled depressed, "crazy," lazy, or malingering, because no organic cause could be found for their suffering. Others were finally able to overcome their own feelings of guilt or the belief that they might have brought on the symptoms themselves as a consequence of self medicating with alcohol or other substances. This sense of relief prevailed even in cases when the diagnosis was extremely grave, as was the case for patients in our study. For them, finally receiving a diagnosis, especially a genetically based one, reduced uncertainty by providing a set of parameters for all to better understand and relate to their situations. This reduction of uncertainty was, ironically, in many cases far more meaningful for the patients (during the period of our study) than the objective gravity of the diagnosis.

We had expected *fatalism* to be another common response to a genetic diagnosis because such a diagnosis is commonly regarded as something immutable. We anticipated that patients given such a diagnosis would perceive it as shutting down their options and otherwise closing doors. This is certainly the case in the area of fetal diagnosis, where finding anything genetically anomalous in a developing fetus is invariably "bad news" for the parents, since nothing can be done to correct the anomaly detected. But instead, we found that a genetic diagnosis could augur hope – at least in the short run, and that, like any other, a genetic diagnosis could be seen as an empowering step toward prevention, treatment, or cure. We saw great faith, however blind, reposed in the idea that prevention could arrest further deterioration or avert the appearance of symptoms in later generations. Patients and family members were convinced of the efficacy of self-help activities like diet, exercise, and especially positive thinking – seeing faith and hope, in and of themselves – as having therapeutic power. Indeed, although we anticipated that intrinsic to lay views of genetics would be a notion of determinism, instead we found that lay genetics concepts were by no means deterministic and in fact, proved to be surprisingly complex. We also expected family issues would be very salient (after all, that's what comes to mind when we talk about something being "in the genes"). But again, we didn't find family issues to be all that central to patients' concerns. Far more important was coming to terms with the consequences of their progressive loss of independence and associated identity-related issues.

Finally, rather than assuming that a diagnosis derived from genetic testing would hold greater "truth value" – or be somehow more legitimating – than a clinical diagnosis based upon a study of the signs and symptoms of a disease, we wanted to understand the actual significance of a genetic diagnosis for the patients, family caregivers, and clinicians in this investigation. We were also interested in the circumstances in which these clinicians sought to diagnose a patient's medical problems based on symptoms and clinical signs, and when they used genetic testing. Following a discussion of how we went about obtaining and analyzing our data and a brief overview of our more general findings, these main themes will be more fully developed.

How we conducted the research

Our research objective was to understand the potential or actual significance of using newly developed genetic tests as they helped patients, family members, and neurologists in illuminating the cause of the patient's symptoms. More broadly, we were interested in the meanings that genetic information created for those involved in the medical experience of dealing with neurodegenerative disease.

Due to the paucity of research on the subject, our study was conceptualized as a hypothesis-generating rather than hypothesis-testing investigation. We therefore sought to develop a diverse, heterogeneous study population that reflected the broad demographics, diagnosis, and treatment options for neurology patients living in a large Western state. Through our own professional networks, we contacted neurologists who treat movement disorders asking if they would allow us to recruit patients for our study; their participation would also require their willingness to allow us to observe these patients' consultations (assuming, of course, the patient's agreement) as well as participation in a 45-minute face-to-face interview.[3] Thirteen neurologists agreed to participate in the research. Among our key objectives were to explore the range of medical contexts in which movement disorder patients in a major U.S. metropolitan area receive care, and to evaluate the impact of practice setting on clinical practices. We therefore sought to include neurologists who worked in private, hospital-based, and neurogenetics specialty clinics. Although it had once been assumed that physicians' clinical practices were essentially homogeneous due to the uniformity of medical school curricula, in recent years, researchers have revealed important variability in those practices (Chavez *et al.* 1995; Lock 1995).

Patients were invited to participate in this investigation if they were seeking a neurological consultation for movement disorder symptoms, as defined earlier, to include progressive loss of strength, muscle mass and mechanical range of motion, slowness or lack of movement, difficulty initiating movement, and effectuating additional or amplified movements. Because there was no way to know prior to the consultation whether the patient already had, would ask for, or would be offered genetic testing, all new patients who reported one or more of the above-described symptoms were recruited. Those with no direct experience with genetic testing became part of our comparison group.

We used four complementary methodological strategies to collect our data: focused observations in clinical settings such as doctors' offices; semi-structured interviews; longitudinal, in-depth interviewing; and participant observation mainly in homes and neighborhoods settings (e.g. picking up kids at school, grocery shopping), and occasionally at other informal venues (e.g. family dinners, weddings, baptisms). This breadth and diversity of approaches reflected our need to adapt standard ethnographic approaches developed for small-scale societies to problem-focused medical anthropological research in urban settings. While conventional ethnography requires that the researcher become immersed in a whole community's daily life over an extended time period, this was neither feasible nor amenable to producing very fruitful findings for this study because urban life is much more fragmented, with each person's experiences more individualized than in smaller-scale settings. Moreover, as more anthropologists have shifted from community studies to urban problem-focused research, our data are more apt to come from larger, more randomly drawn samples, and generally consist of self-reported accounts of behavior elicited during one-time interviews. This contrasts with the hallmarks of traditional ethnography – informal interviews, opportunistic contacts, and participant observation. Nonetheless, as ethnographers, we have the same research goals as ever, as well as the need to find new approaches required for data gathering. These methods helped us to better perceive contradictions between participants' accounts of their experiences and our own observations, as well as to be more sensitive to inconsistencies in situations when their descriptions of their experiences changed over time.

In an effort to ameliorate these dilemmas, we developed some of our own methodological techniques. For example, for the observations, we recorded the content of the clinical consultation using modifications of two paper-and-pencil instruments we originally designed and used successfully in several earlier investigations (Preloran, Browner, and Lieber 2005). The instruments provided a template for recording who was present during the consultation, what interaction occurred, including the factual information volunteered and elicited, questions asked and answered (or not answered), and any obvious emotional reactions we observed.

We subsequently interviewed the patient and, when possible, any accompanying family members, in either English or Spanish, using semi-structured interview guides. The interviews took between 30 minutes and two hours. Data from the first ten interviews were analyzed and, when necessary, questions were revised for completeness, comprehensibility, and effectiveness at eliciting relevant and meaningful information, and then used for the remaining 106 patient and 49 family caregiver interviews. Interview data was tape recorded, transcribed, and translated by us from Spanish to English when needed. Standard field note procedures were followed for the data obtained from participant observations. Interview and observational data were coded qualitatively for themes and quantitatively using the Statistical Package for the Social Sciences (Norusis 2008).

From the interview sample we selected a "nested" sub-sample of patients, and when possible, one or more family members for sustained follow-up in person, by telephone, or email. While it would be impossible to obtain, let alone analyze in-depth sustained longitudinal data from a large number of study participants, doing so with the nested sub-sample offers the best of both worlds. The in-depth case studies collected over an extended time period (in some cases, up to three years) offered unparalleled insight into the complex and often contradictory realities that can characterize individual experience. They also illuminate aspects of the experiences of the larger study population because the in-depth data generate rich sources of hypothesis testing.

Obtaining in-depth narrative accounts from patients and family members draws on an increasingly common approach in medical anthropology and the other health-related social sciences, as researchers have come to perceive sickness and suffering as providing a window into an individual's broader life experiences (Kleinman 1988). Narratives are stories typically told in casual conversation that usually follow a sequential structure and make a moral point (Cebik 1984; Reissman 1993). They provide explanations or rationalizations for why specific events occurred as well as illuminate the roles of the individual characters in bringing about these events. How someone narrates her or his experiences can illuminate not just the content of memory but, more importantly, how those memories shape present identity and future plans (Good and DelVecchio Good 1994). Illness narratives have been employed to reveal how individuals respond to threatening situations involving painful or otherwise challenging medical decisions (DelVecchio Good *et al.* 1994; Early 1982; Garro and Mattingly 2000; Layne 1996; Rapp 1998; Saris 1995). Narrative accounts that both articulate and mediate a life disruption may restructure an individual's sense of self and of social location (Becker 1997; Reimann and Schütze 1991). Illness narratives, like other narratives, demonstrate some of the ways that individuals' views of themselves and their lives are shaped by culture, while also revealing the role of individual experiences in the creation of cultural knowledge.

identity & future plans

Interpreting those narratives, as "healing dramas" (Mattingly 1998), can offer special insight into these processes as they help us understand who we are by revealing how we see ourselves and how we want to project that self image. The significant features of the narrative form are its "image-rich quality, and its capacity to interweave contradictory pictures and symbols and thus offer contradictory explanations in the very same story" (Mattingly and Garro 1994: 771). In the case studies that follow, the illness narratives were offered spontaneously during the course of the standard semi-structured interview, then retold or elaborated during subsequent conversations. This approach gave study participants opportunities to reflect upon unfulfilled expectations, contradictions, and inconsistencies that would not have been revealed had we relied solely on a more structured one-time interview study design.

To analyze the transcripts, we relied on grounded theory (Glaser and Strauss 1967) and scheme analysis (D'Andrade 1991) to construct a totality from the scattered events recounted during any particular interview and over time. Two researchers (from among the Principal Investigator, Co-Principal Investigator and an assistant) read each transcript and independently made notes that were coded by theme into general categories. During our readings, we noted our reasons for coding each excerpt as we did and compared our notes until coding agreement was attained employing Denzin's "progressive-regressive" method of interpretation (Denzin 1989). This involved working both backwards and forwards from an event in order to understand what it represented to the narrator. As themes emerged, they were grouped into meaningful clusters. In doing so, we focused on the "dramatic plot" (Mattingly 1998) of each illness narrative in which participants recounted events that were meaningful with reference to their illness and medical experience within the context of their past, present, and expected or anticipated future life situations. After multiple reviews of each person's transcripts, a number of categories emerged representing the issues that the participant repeatedly emphasized throughout our encounters.

Structure of the book

Before turning to the qualitative analyses drawn from the nested sub-sample in the succeeding chapters, we offer a summary of our quantitative findings. This overview will provide context for the in-depth case studies and foreground broader patterns in the data. Quantitative analyses like these can also help the reader understand which aspects of our case studies are atypical or even idiosyncratic and which reflect more global patterns in the data and have generalizable significance.

The six qualitative chapters to follow are organized into three sections: Parts I and II each consist of accounts of the medical experiences, and surrounding family and social experiences, of individual patients. Chapters 1 and 2 offer detailed analyses of two patients' long and arduous efforts to discover the cause of their neurodegenerative symptoms. Their stories are broadly illustrative of our larger study population, who were impelled to continue seeking new medical information until they were convinced that their diagnosis accurately reflected their own experience with their disease. Chapters 3 and 4 offer the narratives of two other patients, who, after years of searching, finally receive definitive diagnoses for their movement disorder symptoms through genetic testing, but then find the diagnoses only lead to new questions. We consider the impact and meaning of their diagnoses for these patients' identities and subsequent life plans. In Part III we step back from the extended case study approach to draw more comprehensively on our family and clinician samples. Chapter 5 highlights the diversity of family caregivers' experiences with patients suffering chronic progressive neurodegenerative symptoms within the contexts of genetic testing and genetic diagnoses. We show that while some strove to help their relatives restore or at least sustain their deteriorating health and pre-illness identities, others attempted to "stand-in" for their relatives in order to move on with their own lives. Still others ignored their relatives' needs altogether. Chapter 6 explores the views and experiences of the 13 neurologists who participated in our investigation. We focus on what they perceive to be the significance of genetic testing for patients with neurodegenerative movement disorder symptoms and whether such tests address and diminish their own anxieties about the current limitations of the field of neurology for accurately diagnosing and actually treating patients with neurodegenerative disease.

Study participants

Between February 2004 and March 2007, we observed 125 new patient intakes. Of them, 92 percent were part of our purposive sample drawn from six medical facilities: just over a third at the general neurology clinic at a county hospital, 32 percent at two universities and one research institution, and 27 percent at two private neighborhood clinics. Like most ethnographers, we sought to obtain data from the widest range of relevant settings. Therefore, an additional 8 percent of the observations were opportunistically obtained at other private clinics.

Of the 125 clinical encounters observed, we were able to interview 116 patients. In addition, we opportunistically interviewed nine patients without having observed their clinical consultation. Forty-seven of the 71 patients who were accompanied by a relative to their consultation agreed to an interview. As already noted, we also interviewed 13 neurologists, neurology fellows, and residents, along with four medical assistants and one genetic counselor concerning the broad research questions, their experiences working in specific types of clinical settings, and their experiences with those patients who were also part of the patient study population.

One quarter (n = 31) of the patients had either already undergone genetic testing before entering our study or who were offered such testing during the course of our research. They and their family members were asked their views about and experiences with genetic testing. The rest, our comparison group, were asked a series of hypothetical questions on the same subjects. We compare the responses of the testing-offered and hypothetical-testing groups. The case studies we offer for in-depth qualitative analysis are all part of the group who were offered genetic testing.

The patient group was roughly balanced by gender, with slightly more men (n = 64) than women (n = 61). Patients' ages ranged from 18 to 94 (mean = 56.04,

S.D. = 17.82); with the women, on average, just a little older (mean = 56.98, S.D. = 17.08) than the men (mean = 55.14, S.D. = 18.59). In contrast, the family caregivers were overwhelmingly female (n = 38), with very few males (n = 9) participating. They ranged in age from 17 to 80 (mean = 45.94; S.D. = 16.02); with the women again tending to be older (mean = 46.45; S.D. = 16.14) than the men (mean = 43.78; S.D. = 16.28). Just over half the family members interviewed were the patients' children, 21 percent were spouses, 15 percent siblings, 9 percent parents, and 4 percent nieces.

Most patients were born either in the U.S. (39 percent) or in Mexico (41 percent); the rest (20 percent) were from Central America (El Salvador, Guatemala), South America (Ecuador, Colombia, Argentina, Chile, Peru, Uruguay), the Caribbean (Jamaica, Cuba), Asia (China, Korea, the Philippines), Africa (Ethiopia), Europe (France) and the Middle East (Iran). Nearly all were raised in the country where they were born, with 90 percent of the immigrants having come to the U.S. as adults, after the age of 18.

Like the patients, most relatives hailed from Mexico (43 percent) or the U.S. (38 percent); the remainder were born in Central America (El Salvador), South America (Argentina, Uruguay), Asia (China), the Caribbean (Jamaica), and Europe (Italy). Nearly all (94 percent) were raised in their country of origin, and most (68 percent), although a smaller proportion than the patients, immigrated after the age of 18.

Native-born patients and family members had significantly more education than the immigrants and were much more likely to have white-collar or professional employment. Of the 49 percent of patients who had not completed high school, fully 90 percent were born outside the U.S. The 20 percent of patients who had only a high school education were nearly evenly split between immigrants and U.S. natives; in contrast, over three quarters of the 32 percent who had attended and/or graduated from college were U.S.-born. The pattern was similar for relatives. And whether U.S.- or foreign-born, both patients' and family members' occupational histories were generally consistent with their levels of education.

The overwhelming majority of patients (78 percent) had children and, in some cases, grandchildren, but only 6 percent reported that their offspring had health problems similar to their own and just three patients said that their child also suffered from an adult-onset movement disorder. However, nearly one-quarter of the patients said they had other relatives who also suffered movement disorder symptoms. The results for family members about their children, their children's health, and that of their relatives were similar. Most patients lived with at least one other person; only 20 percent lived alone. The majority (53 percent) lived with a caregiver (most often their spouse or child), with or without other family members.

Experiences with neurodegenerative symptoms

In recounting how their neurological symptoms were affecting their daily lives, two-thirds of the patients indicated that the inexorable loss of their independence was the hardest burden to bear. Others were most affected by what they described as a relentless emotional drain or the demoralizing effects of their illness on other family members. A minority reported that the worst consequences were the uncertainty about their prognoses, the financial burden of their illness, and ceaseless worries about whether their insurance coverage would remain sufficient.

Despite their movement disorder symptoms, which for many were quite devastating, and in some cases already found to be genetic and in others a strong possibility, we saw little evidence of fatalism or resignation. Instead, most patients sought to remain as actively engaged as possible in their own medical care. The most common types of self-help activities reported were: following physicians' recommendations such as taking prescribed medications (69 percent); prayer (36 percent); exercise (15 percent); and talking with friends (10 percent). Just 13 percent said that there was not much they could do for themselves in the area of self-care. These findings are consistent with research by Chapple, May, and Campion who, in a study of families who sought genetic counseling at one clinic in the north of England, found that despite study participants' recognition that many diseases were caused by genetic factors, they nevertheless believed in the efficacy of self-help activities (Chapple, May, and Campion 1995). Di Prospero and her associates report a similar pattern: "Despite the lack of scientific evidence that diet or lifestyle changes can alter the risk of cancer in people with the *BRCA* mutation, our study population expressed high confidence in the effectiveness of such changes" (Di Prospero *et al.* 2001:1008).

To further explore the experience of living with movement disorder symptoms, we asked family members what they found most challenging about caring for their sick relative. Most talked principally about the emotional toll of caring for someone with a progressive disease: the relentless nature of their relative's worsening medical condition (52 percent), the heartbreak of seeing them deteriorate to such an extent that it was like caring for a child (36 percent), an ongoing uncertainty about their relative's prognosis (33 percent), and fears they too could one day find themselves in the same situation (27 percent). Smaller, but substantial proportions said they found most challenging the amount of time required to care for their relative (33 percent), the financial burden of the illness (27 percent), and worries about insurance coverage (18 percent). Still, most family members had developed strategies to deal with the stresses of caring for their relatives; talking with friends (45 percent) and prayer (25 percent) being most frequently mentioned. Nearly one-quarter (22 percent) said that there was not much they could do to lighten their burden.

Clinical experiences with genetic testing

We observed medical evaluations in three types of clinical settings in which patients might have been offered genetic testing in the course of their current diagnostic evaluations for their neurodegenerative symptoms: solo practice private neighborhood walk-in clinics, which we will refer to as "neighborhood clinics"; general neurology clinics located in a large public hospital and a university medical center, which we will call "institution-based clinics"; and neurogenetics specialty clinics based in public and private research facilities, which we will refer to as "specialty clinics."

Despite relatively minor variation, notably on the dimensions of the amount of time a patient spent waiting to see the physician and the number of medical personnel with whom the patient interacted, regardless of practice setting the content of these consultations were quite standard (cf. Roter and Hall 1992). In the neighborhood clinics, the clinical encounter generally began with a nurse or receptionist ushering the patient and anyone accompanying the patient into a small examination room. A short while later, the neurologist entered, greeted the patient, and conducted the consultation, beginning by ascertaining the reason for the consultation and then taking the patient's clinical history, performing a physical examination, which would include a brief neurological evaluation (e.g. walking a given number of steps, balancing on one foot, reflexes, etc.), ordering tests, and making a clinical plan.

In the institution-based settings, after a nurse weighed the patient and took vital signs, the remaining aforementioned tasks were performed by a resident physician, who would then leave the examination room to consult with the supervising attendant physician and return to offer a treatment plan. In the case of monolingual study participants, the consultation was conducted with the aid of an interpreter, usually a member of the clinic staff.

At the specialty clinics, a nurse similarly first weighed the patient and also took vital signs. Next, a neurology resident or fellow determined the patient's reasons for seeking a consultation, took a detailed medical history, conducted an extensive physical examination intended to evaluate the severity of the patient's movement disorder and other possibly related symptoms (e.g. memory loss, depression), and noted any drugs and supplements the patient was currently taking. Upon completing these tasks, the junior physician left to consult with the attending, and together they returned, sometimes accompanied by one or more medical students or other physicians. The attending physician either repeated some of the same questions or asked a small number of new ones and then reprised selected aspects of the general physical exam or a more specialized movement disorder assessment.

At this point, given that most patients in this study were seeking second, third or subsequent medical opinions, a diagnosis or some tentative explanation of the cause of the patient's symptoms (e.g. exposure to toxic substances, family history, vitamin deficiencies, etc.) might be offered. However, more often, the patient was referred for various types of additional tests (e.g. blood, urine, scans), including in some cases, genetic tests, and was asked to schedule a follow up appointment to further discuss diagnosis and prognosis. A change in the patient's medication was also sometimes prescribed: either the incorporation of different drugs or supplements or an adjustment in the dosage of drugs currently taken. Physical and/or speech therapy were also sometimes prescribed. In most cases, actual interaction between patient and doctor lasted from 10 to 45 minutes.

When we asked the participating neurologists how, in principal, they determined whether a movement disorder patient was an appropriate candidate for genetic testing, most said their decision was based on the patient's medical history and the availability of suitable tests. We found, however, that additional factors, notably clinicians' perception as to whether the patient could afford the cost of testing (or would be eligible for free testing), as well as how meaningful they thought the results would be to the patient were also considerations. To make this assessment, we compared those who had had genetic testing with those who had not. We found that as a group, those who were offered testing were statistically significantly older, more likely to have been born and raised in the U.S., and more likely to have completed high school. However, the most important factor determining whether patients were offered genetic testing was where they received their medical care: patients recruited at the university and research institutions were two and a half times more likely than those at the county hospital and five times more likely than those at the neighborhood clinics to be offered genetic testing.

Shifting our focus from neurologists, we looked at patients' and family caregivers' knowledge of genetics and their attitudes about genetic testing. Despite clear differences in their knowledge about genetics and genetic testing to diagnose movement disorder symptoms, comparing patients who had been offered genetic testing (i.e. the testing-offered group) and their relatives with those who had not been (i.e. the hypothetical-testing group), we found that neither group was particularly well informed. Just 62 percent of patients and 71 percent of relatives in the testing-offered group said they were aware of such tests prior to being offered them. This compares with just 28 percent of patients and 25 percent of relatives in the hypothetical-testing group. These marked differences of awareness about genetic testing did not greatly surprise us. They seemed to show that at least some type of informed consent process had accompanied the offer of genetic testing. More interesting was the fact that only 62 percent of the patients who had undergone genetic testing reported that they had been aware of the existence of genetic tests for their symptoms prior to being tested (a few even remained unaware after having been tested). This was consistent with our observations. Clinicians generally offered the tests as simply another diagnostic tool and tended not to encourage discussion about any larger implications that positive genetic test results can have. This is shown clearly below and will be developed in more detail in some of the following chapters that focus on patient case studies, but particularly in Chapter 6, "The neurologists' conundrum."

The most common sources of information about genetics and genetic testing to help diagnose movement disorder symptoms for both groups of patients were similar, and in order of frequency: relatives and friends (38 percent), television (22 percent), online sources (19 percent), books, magazines, and pamphlets (16 percent), and physicians (13 percent). (Interestingly, physicians came in last.)

Most patients (82 percent) and relatives (70 percent) who talked with their neurologist about genetic testing reported little difficulty understanding them, and most patients (73 percent) and relatives (91 percent) were aware that a positive genetic diagnosis generally meant that the condition had a hereditary cause or component. There was less agreement between the testing-offered and hypothetical-testing groups as to whether a genetic diagnosis would lead to more effective treatments for them personally: nearly two-thirds of the testing-offered group of patients and all but one of the relatives (93 percent) said that no cure was available, compared with just 13 percent of the hypothetical-testing patient and 42 percent of their relative group. These differences may indicate that those who had had genetic testing may have received more information than those who did not.

Although only 11 percent of the hypothetical-testing group said they thought that their illness might be hereditary, over three-fourths said they would nevertheless undergo genetic testing if it could tell them for sure. This is similar to Meiser and associates' finding that most participants in a study of families with a history of bipolar disorder said they would be interested in genetic testing if it gave a definitive diagnosis (Meiser *et al*. 2005:115). Still, just 26 percent of patients in our study and 50 percent of relatives said they would encourage their children and grandchildren to be tested. Reasons for not recommending testing included the belief that it would not lead to better treatment, that the results could be upsetting, lead to discrimination, or negatively affect family dynamics. The most common reasons given by the minority who would recommend such testing to children and grandchildren included the possibility of early treatment, the reduction of uncertainty, and going along if the doctor suggested it.

Given the entire study population's overall lack of general knowledge on the subject of genetic testing, it is not surprising that most study participants were, for the most part, unaware of the intense debates that have been waged for more than two decades about the extent to which genetic testing raises any special psychological, social, or bioethical concerns (Duster 1990; Lippman 1991; Rapp 2000). Only minorities of both the testing-offered and the hypothetical-testing patient (15 percent and 13 percent respectively) and family groups (13 percent and 42 percent) felt that genetic testing did, indeed, pose special concerns (Hallowell *et al*. 2003; Sharpe and Carter 2006a). The most common concerns mentioned by patients were potential negative mental health consequences, financial burdens associated with the cost of testing, increased risk of insurance discrimination, and possible family conflicts. Most often mentioned by relatives were fears of insurance discrimination, cost of the tests, and concerns about the effect of bad news on the patient's mental health. Other researchers have similarly found that while many are generally aware of the existence of genetic testing, for the most part they are not overly concerned about stereotyping, stigma or discrimination that could result from a genetic diagnosis (Davis and Ponsaran 2008).

The vast majority of patients offered genetic testing (81 percent) accepted, and most agreed on the spot to be tested. The six patients who took time to decide gave diverse reasons including wanting to consider the costs of testing, fear of potential discrimination, concern about potential impact on other family members, and wanting time to elicit support for their decision. Surprisingly, few of the patients offered genetic testing (just 14 percent) said they had been referred to a genetic counselor either before or after being tested.

Most, but not all of the patients (77 percent) said they told close friends and/or relatives after being tested. They reported that the large majority (87 percent) of the family and friends who were informed said they felt that the patient had made the right decision. Similarly, all of the interviewed relatives of patients who agreed to genetic testing said they thought the patient had decided correctly about having been tested.

We found it instructive to compare the views and experiences of patients who had actually undergone genetic testing and their relatives, with the hypothetical-testing groups on questions about how the latter imagined they would respond if they or their relatives were offered genetic testing for their current problems. We consistently noted strong differences in the responses of the two groups. For instance, in answer to the question "Whose opinion should have the most weight in reaching a decision?," 74 percent of the genetic testing-offered group said their own had been most important, while just 52 percent of the hypothetical-testing group imagined that would be the case for them. Correspondingly, 92 percent of the hypothetical-testing group said the opinions of close family members would be very important in making a genetic testing decision, contrasting sharply with just 24 percent of testing-offered patients who indicated they had taken the opinions of close family members into account.

This pattern seems to indicate that differences between the genetic testing-offered group and hypothetical-testing groups on this dimension were due to actual experience with genetic testing: those who actually had gone through the decision-making process knew that in the end their decision had been their own, whereas those who did not may have imagined that should they be offered the opportunity, they might not have the capacity to decide and would have to rely on family to determine the best course of action.

We also found differences between the two family caregiver groups in their answers to the same question. Half the family members in the hypothetical-testing group indicated that the patient's opinion should have the most weight in deciding about genetic testing, contrasting significantly with only 31 percent of relatives in the testing-offered group. In the testing-offered relative group 31 percent also reported that it had been their opinion that had been most important, while just 10 percent of the hypothetical-testing relative group imagined this would be the case if their own relative were to be offered genetic testing. Although just one relative in the hypothetical-testing group indicated that the opinion of the patient's doctor should have the most weight in such a decision, 39 percent of the testing-offered relative group told us this had been the case in their own relative's situation.

While the genetic test results of the majority of patients (54 percent) were positive, meaning that their condition had a genetic cause or component, a substantial minority was negative (31 percent) or inconclusive (15 percent). Still, regardless of outcome, most patients (75 percent) and relatives (57 percent) said that the test result had not materially changed their views of themselves or feelings about the illness.

These statistical findings came as a surprise. Our informal conversations with a number of patients while they were waiting for the results of genetic testing led us to believe that should they receive a genetic diagnosis, they would regard it as "more accurate" – some said even transformational. As we shall see in the chapters in Part II, some patients did make major life changes following their genetic diagnosis. These results offer some contrast with work by Lock and associates with close relatives of patients diagnosed with Alzheimer's disease who reported few if any meaningful changes in their sense of identity or their lifestyles following their own genetic testing (Lock *et al.* 2007). Differences in the findings from the two studies may be explained in part by the fact that the research by Lock and her colleagues was with asymptomatic relatives, whereas ours was with actual patients. Our results also exemplify the difference between the responses individuals may give to hypothetical questions that ask them to project into an imagined future versus their experience when actually finding themselves in that hypothetical situation. Nevertheless, a sense that something could perhaps be done should they receive a genetic diagnosis – if not right now, at some later time – could be the reason why the large majority (77 percent) of patients said that they would recommend genetic testing to someone with similar symptoms.

Aims of the book

We found this study of neurodegenerative disease to be among the most complex we have ever undertaken. It placed in sharp relief the limitations of early twenty-first-century medical care: diagnostic limitations, unsuccessful treatments, dramatic and continually escalating disruptions of identities and lives. This book aims to highlight some of these issues. In so doing, we move beyond a narrow focus on the actual use of genetic testing to broader aspects of the medical experience, reflecting on the ways in which neurodegenerative disorders challenge and ultimately transform patients' and their families' medical, social, and personal situations, and how genetic information contributes to these journeys of transformation. Most of the patients we encountered had actively sought medical answers for their neurological symptoms for many years. The answers they had gotten, if any, were often ambiguous and frequently devastating. Yet despite suspicions and fears that their symptoms reflected the inexorable course of a progressively deteriorating disease, many continued their search for even more specific diagnoses and/or better treatment – searches that often proved fruitless.

In an effort to comprehensively chart patients' struggles to find the causes of, and prognoses for, their debilitating symptoms, we next present illustrative case studies from our sample. We'll show that although some patients were ultimately successful in obtaining the medical information they were seeking, the gravity of their diagnosis was often far more serious than they had imagined. And moreover, that in obtaining the diagnostic certainty that had long eluded them, new questions emerged, the answers to which only heightened their original fears. Yet even at these most vexing junctures, patients still reached out for help, striving to improve their health and maintain their self-dignity. These courageous patients and their family caregivers' strategies for persevering and adjusting to a new life – despite ominous storm clouds looming overhead – are this book's greatest inspiration.

Part I

Searching for answers

Searching for answers documents two patients' protracted and arduous efforts to discover the cause of their symptoms, and the consequences after each received a genetic test result: one negative and the other positive. Their stories are broadly illustrative of our larger study population, many of whom were impelled to continue seeking new medical information until they were convinced that their diagnoses accurately reflected their own experience with their disease.

For patients suffering with neurodegenerative movement disorder symptoms, finding an accurate diagnosis can be complex because most associated symptoms occur in a number of different diseases; only a few can be diagnosed with an objective test, genetic or otherwise. In this regard, diagnosis in neurology shares much with psychiatry: the same symptoms may appear in several distinct conditions and arriving at an accurate diagnosis is often based mainly, if not entirely, on a patient's description of his or her symptoms and the clinician's judgment and prior experience treating other patients with similar symptoms (Young 1997). Therefore many neurodegenerative patients' and relatives' newfound hopes that genetic testing will produce the long-elusive definitive diagnosis are often met with disappointment, and they continue to endure years of worsening symptoms.

We focus first on Liz Morgan,[1] a 53-year-old accountant from a European-American background. Motivated by seeing close relatives end their lives in wheelchairs without ever receiving accurate diagnoses, Liz fought to maintain her trust in a medical system that ultimately failed to offer her conclusive answers, even with genetic testing. Liz's health continued to deteriorate during the two years of our acquaintance, and while she remained generally satisfied with her doctors, she lost her trust in their ability to find any new effective treatments, let alone a meaningful diagnosis. By the end of our acquaintance, Liz had decided to discontinue all mainstream medical care, although she was undecided as to whether to pursue alternative medicine as her husband was urging. Her story illuminates the important but often overlooked distinction in the different roles that satisfaction and trust play in patients' clinical experiences: while Liz remained satisfied with the quality of the care she was receiving, she lost trust in the power of biomedicine to satisfy her quest for information and improvement, or even to simply maintain her level of health. This awakening precipitated a profound sense of hopelessness for what the future would hold.

We will also meet Ana Almendra, a 37-year-old Mexican American woman who introduced herself to us as "the mother of two beautiful children." Her own mother described her daughter as "living in a world of fears," an edifice that had been elaborately constructed out of her childhood sufferings and her adult experiences with her father's erratic and disturbing behavior and his ultimate death from Huntington's disease. Ana's story highlights the analytical distinction between "illness," a patient's embodied perceptions, and "disease," clinicians' objective findings and assessments (Boorse 2004). It also illuminates how communication between doctor and patient becomes problematic when each seeks to understand the meaning of the same symptoms but approaches them through distinct or even divergent paradigms. We show that even Ana's case, with her clear family history of a dread disease, was no exception, and how and why communication broke down entirely when the discrepancy between her illness experiences and the disease her clinicians were treating overwhelmed the meaning of their interactions.

For years, Ana had believed that she was suffering from the same neurodegenerative condition that destroyed the life of her estranged father, but those fears were dismissed by clinicians and even by her family, most of whom were convinced that her symptoms were mostly, if not entirely, imagined. Sadly, Ana's fears proved correct: a genetic test revealed that she carried the gene for Huntington's disease. Within a year of receiving this diagnosis, Ana's symptoms began to manifest in ways that frightened her all the more, but even then their relationship to Huntington's disease continued to be questioned by her doctors.

1   A new door opening

When we met Liz Morgan, like many study participants, she had been traveling a long, bumpy road in search of a diagnosis, and consistently coming up "empty handed," with inconclusive or even contradictory medical opinions. Liz was typical of our larger study population, optimistically believing that if she persevered, she would eventually discover the root cause of her symptoms. But the lengths to which she was willing to go to get meaningful answers were extreme. As we became more acquainted with Liz, we saw her strong sense of determination as she scheduled neurological evaluations at two different specialty clinics (referred to here as Clinic A and Clinic B) during a ten-day period, with the single goal of finally getting a definitive diagnosis, hopefully through genetic testing. We were excited to encounter this rare opportunity to observe how practitioners with similar training working in different clinical settings evaluated the same patient at a common point in time. This fortuitous circumstance, combined with Liz's willingness to participate in our study "for as long as necessary," led us to invite her to join our in-depth sample. We followed her case for more than two years.

The ways in which trust and satisfaction influence patients' medical experiences in the case of short-term illnesses have been studied extensively (Hall *et al.* 2001; Mechanic 1996). But far less attention has been paid to patients with chronic and deteriorating medical conditions without diagnoses and with uncertain prognoses. Moreover, most research on the impact of severe illness has focused on family dynamics, economic factors, and the disruption of everyday life (Power and Dell Orto 2004; Rolland 1994), or on how dimensions such as socioeconomic background, ethnicity, age, and gender may inhibit or enhance treatment opportunities and experiences (Siegrist 1999; Waitzkin 2000). In contrast, Liz's case opened a window onto the devastating effects of temporality on patients as they struggled for years with progressive degenerative diseases with inconclusive diagnoses and without effective treatments. Liz's story provided a chance to explore how a patient's trust in the medical system can be maintained – as well as how and why it may collapse.

Our data come from four in-person meetings and five telephone conversations. Liz's husband, Paul, was present at two of our meetings, although he said little and declined our request for a private interview, explaining that he was overwhelmed trying to avoid bankruptcy and salvaging the family's money problems after some serious financial "missteps" by his wife. Tragically, the year before we met the couple, Paul had been diagnosed with a life threatening form of cancer.

Liz's search for answers

We were introduced to Liz in the waiting room of Medical Center A's neurogenetics specialty clinic (Clinic A) by one of our participating neurologists. She had been referred there to confirm a clinical diagnosis[1] of a hereditary ataxia, whose main symptoms include impaired coordination of movement, degenerative changes in the brain and spinal cord and wide-based gait. At this first meeting, Liz volunteered that her neurodegenerative symptoms were affecting her to the extent that she was no longer sure of "who [she was]." She also wanted us to understand that despite her present limitations, she had at one time been a successful accountant and a brilliant investor. She had been married to Paul, an electrical engineer, for almost 30 years. The couple had no children. Liz, in her mid-fifties and Paul, age 60, were both natives of the large metropolitan area where we conducted much of our research.

Liz and Paul had grown up in working-class families and were proud that after a lifetime of hard work, they had ascended into the middle class; both agreed that Liz's investment skills had been the key to their economic success. Hopes for a bright future and years of comfortable retirement abruptly vanished when both were forced to stop working due to illness.

Choosing a clinic

As we were getting acquainted while waiting for her consultation at Clinic A to begin, Liz offered some history and context for her medical visit that day: "When I heard I could have a hereditary ataxia . . . I ran to the internet because it was an illness I'd never heard of before," she explained. There she found descriptions of the different ataxias along with the names of neurologists in her area who were specialists in treating that type of condition. She elected to see a doctor at Medical Center B's clinic (Clinic B), where she was put on an appointment waiting list of more than a year. Disappointed but undaunted, she also booked an appointment at Clinic A, "because [she] knew that . . . both were the best [around]."

Liz's experience at Clinic A started out well enough. She visited their general neurology clinic five times for evaluations and drug management and was generally satisfied with the care. She reported having developed a rapport with the clinicians and trust in their initial clinical diagnosis of hereditary ataxia. She was pleased to have been referred to a specialist in neurogenetics to confirm the clinical assessment. She was hopeful that the consultation would offer more "precise" answers along with new information about her condition, prognosis, and how to best manage her symptoms.

27 June: consultation at specialty Clinic A

Paul accompanied Liz to the consultation, as he did to all her medical appointments. She quickly agreed to let us sit in on the evaluation and to subsequently meet with her for additional conversations. While we were still in the waiting room, she volunteered that she was very excited to finally be having a "genetic evaluation" because she did not want to end up like her relatives, passively living out their days "in wheelchairs not knowing what was going on in their bodies." Liz told us she recognized that one day she could find herself in a similar situation and was determined to find a treatment, firmly stating, "It doesn't matter what it [will] take."

Dr Weiss, a research fellow, opened the consultation by asking Liz the reason for her visit. She replied, "I want to confirm my diagnosis of a hereditary ataxia, cerebellum [ataxia], or something like that." She volunteered that she had been a successful accountant until she began to have problems with speech, memory loss, and lack of coordination that eventually caused her to go on disability leave a year earlier.

As the consultation continued, Liz responded clearly to Dr Weiss's questions and detailed her journey in search of a "precise" diagnosis that had begun three years earlier when she started experiencing problems walking. She said she had received an inconclusive diagnosis from her general practitioner and had subsequently lost track of the number of specialists she consulted thereafter. Paul offered that they might have had "more than twenty consultations in the last couple of years." Liz added that her perseverance was grounded in her assumption that an accurate diagnosis would set her on the right path, "If I at least knew what is wrong, I could start to work on it and things would get better."

She then admitted that despite her months of positive experiences at specialty Clinic A, she had not canceled a previously made appointment at the neurogenetics specialty Clinic B. The young doctor smiled as Liz continued, "And something miraculous happened. [Someone at Clinic B] called announcing a cancellation and offering me the opening in ten days." Liz told Dr Weiss she hoped he would not mind that she would be seeking another opinion. He responded, "It's perfectly all right with me," to which Liz exclaimed, "If all of you [doctors at both clinics] agree, then we can be sure we are on the right track."

As Dr Weiss took down Liz's medical history, we learned that her father had suffered what Liz described as a similar tremor in his hands, memory loss, and coordination problems when walking. She also reported that her father had never received a formal diagnosis for his illness. She added that her only brother also suffered from memory loss, coordination problems, and progressive difficulties with his speech, and that he, like his father before him, had ended up in a wheelchair. Liz asked Dr Weiss whether he thought that the symptoms she was experiencing along with those visible in her brother could be due to obesity or if it was more likely "something we got from our father who never passed on anything of value to us, anyway." Dr Weiss's response was noncommittal: "Well . . . obesity doesn't help [and] I don't know your brother . . ."

The consultation followed previously described standardized protocol as Dr Weiss evaluated Liz's movement and mental capabilities. As the evaluation seemed to be drawing to a close, Liz returned to earlier topics, repeating three times that her memory problems "drive everybody crazy" and "get [her] into trouble." Among other lapses, she reported that she had forgotten to pay their mortgage several times and that as a result the couple was in danger of losing their home.

Dr Weiss seemed to be attentive, making frequent eye contact with both Liz and Paul and nodding as if he was following the conversation. Still, the overall interactional dynamic felt somewhat formal. Towards the end of the history intake, Dr Weiss asked Liz if she had anything more she wanted to add. She remained silent until Paul encouraged her to say what was on her mind. Looking spent Liz gathered her energies before relating in a sad and somber tone that she felt as though her health was deteriorating more and more rapidly. She was most worried about the fact that her memory problems seemed to be worsening and she sensed she was losing her ability to speak. Then, mustering newfound energy and speaking more loudly, she reiterated her determination to use whatever energy and resources she still had "to get to the bottom of things" because she was growing more convinced that she was "losing it."

During the physical assessment, Liz stumbled after just one step, failing to reach the designated target. She was also unable to maintain her balance while standing. She asked again if obesity could be the cause of her motor problems since she was 100 pounds heavier than she had been when she began to have balance and walking problems. Dr Weiss repeated that while obesity didn't help, it should not be considered the cause of her problem. At this point Liz asked for the third time whether the origin of her illness could be hereditary, to which the doctor replied, "It could be, but I doubt it." A long, somewhat tense, silence followed.

Although Dr Weiss had just said he did not believe that Liz's problem was genetic, he broke the awkward silence by asking for more information about the medical histories of her relatives. Liz recalled her father: "I remember when I was a child I . . . my brother and I . . . we used to make fun of him because of the way he walked and the tremors in his hands," adding that he died of cancer and never had a neurological evaluation. In response to a question about the family's reproductive history, Liz reported that neither she nor her brother "had reproduced." Later, after Dr Weiss had left the room, she confided that although her lack of children had been a source of sorrow in earlier years, she now viewed it as "a blessing in disguise" because in the event she was diagnosed with a hereditary condition, she would not have put any descendents at risk.

Dr Weiss's departure lasted about 12 minutes before he returned to the examination room accompanied by Dr Barker, a senior attending physician. Dr Barker introduced himself and explained that they had been analyzing Liz's case in-depth. Immediately, Liz perked up and said she was ready to hear their conclusions. Dr Barker responded that he first wanted to perform some additional evaluations and briefly asked Liz some of the same questions Dr Weiss had earlier asked. She repeated her concerns about speech problems, memory loss, and difficulties with concentration, adding that they had rendered her unable to continue working as an accountant. Dr Barker didn't respond directly to any of her concerns. Instead he changed the subject to the drugs Liz was taking and suggested some minor dosage modifications. He concluded by saying that they could not find "anything wrong" with her medications and suggested one more blood test, without specifying what it would evaluate. The previously comfortable tenor in the room shifted sharply as Liz became visibly upset.

Liz: Doctor, for more than a week you've had my chart, you have the
              results of all my tests . . . you have the opinion of my [previous]
              neurologists. [long pause] I answered every one of your questions . . .
              Why can't you tell me something? [long pause] What do you think?
Dr Weiss: [Following a long silence] It's too early to tell. Please be patient a
              little longer.

On that abrupt and inconclusive note, the consultation ended. Both physicians
thanked and said goodbye to the couple, and Dr Barker added that someone would
be in touch with them.

As Liz, her husband, and the ethnographer were alone and preparing to leave,
Paul, who had been silent during most of the consultation, began to talk in a melan-
choly tone. He indicated that he was very worried that Liz's condition would continue to deteriorate and that she might become aggressive like her father had been
in his later years. He added that Liz had already begun to show signs of rudeness
that both hurt and pushed away other people, including him; he also again mentioned their financial troubles. But as Paul was speaking, Liz shook her head as if to
say she did not want to hear anymore. Our immediate attempts to reestablish communication with Liz were unsuccessful and she remained quiet until we said our
goodbyes.

2 July

Liz was in better spirits and more communicative when we spoke by phone. She
began by saying that she had left Clinic A disappointed and frustrated by the lack of
"concrete and precise answers," and added that after six consultations there, she
was losing her faith in the competence of the clinicians. The conversation ended,
however, on an optimistic note when she mentioned her upcoming appointment at
Clinic B: "I feel happy because another door is opening."

During a second phone conversation later that day, Liz repeated that of all the difficulties she was experiencing, she was most troubled by her growing inability to
handle the family's finances:

> This situation is driving me . . . my husband . . . everybody crazy. At the begin-
> ning I thought I could handle it. I wrote notes to myself, I was careful to check
> them every day . . . and keep them in places where I could easily see them. I have
> them close to the phone on my desk and on my bedside table . . . but it seems that
> even though they were there, I would forget to look and, well . . . this is . . . really
> serious. I have forgotten to make important payments – my husband is trying to
> fix it, but we have high penalties and my checkbook is a mess. I don't want to
> think about this, but it's a reality. I can't hide it; I have to face it . . .

Her declining health and escalating economic problems seemed to be Liz's main
concerns. During this same conversation, to help us better understand the weight of
these dual preoccupations she added:

Money is very important for us because we come from working-class families. My husband and I worked hard, very hard, to have what we have . . . He is a good provider, he makes a good living but he always says that it is not the money he made but my investments that got us where we are today . . . Paul had complete trust in me. I was a completely dependable person. And now everything has changed, he has to check on me constantly; that makes me feel horrible. I was a rock and now I'm [silence]. I forget everything, mainly numbers, and what is an accountant without numbers? He needs to check everything – even if I have taken my medicines, even the number of pills the doctors prescribed. It's sad.

Intertwined with and compounding these worries, Liz volunteered that in the last year she felt as though Paul had become emotionally distant. She initially said his behavior was understandable, given that he himself was also in the throes of a very serious illness, but then she quickly added that she believed this new distance was due to "his losing patience with me [in his role as caregiver] and because he's lost trust in me – he thinks I'll keep causing us economic strain." She tried to sound casual, but her voice cracked when she added that now her closest relationship was with her dog.

3 July

Speaking again with Liz by phone, she recounted that she had had a bad night and felt depressed, adding that she was "terrified" she was losing her mental capacities:

I need to get to the bottom of this. I'm sure that if we know what it is, we can do something. I had complete trust in science, but now I've begun to lose it. Last year, especially after going to the best possible [institutions] and coming out empty handed, I began to lose faith. I know that medicine doesn't cure everything but I [also] know that a good diagnosis helps and I assure you that I'll do my best to get it. Luckily I have great insurance through my husband's job, and I hope we'll get a final answer at my next appointment [at Clinic B]. This [hope] is what's keeping me going today.

7 July: consultation at specialty Clinic B

Because Clinics A and B share a similar intake protocol, here we offer only the pieces of information that describe interactions that seemed to have influenced Liz's decision to continue her treatment at Clinic B while ceasing to seek treatment at Clinic A. She had invited us to join her and Paul for her consultation at Clinic B.

While waiting for the consultation to begin, Liz reported being dissatisfied with her final visit to Clinic A, "Although the care was okay . . . I still can't see the light at the end of the tunnel." When asked what "okay" meant she only added, "The doctors were attentive, especially [Dr Weiss]." After a silence, we asked whether anything specific had gone wrong. Liz replied that her main frustration stemmed from the doctors' lack of interest in "the mess" she had made of her financial situation.

Regarding her expectations for the consultation that was about to begin, she said she was "full of hope" adding, "I was close to losing my faith in doctors and medicine but this opportunity made me feel great, I feel a new door is opening."

Just then, the actual door to the examination room did open and Dr Dordoni, a young neurology resident, came in. After introducing herself to the couple, she turned to Liz and exclaimed, "What a beautiful blouse – and so patriotic! It looks like you're still celebrating the Fourth of July!" Both women laughed and continued to engage in casual conversation.

After chatting for several more minutes, Dr Dordoni asked Liz the reason for her visit. As she had at Clinic A, Liz offered an extended explanation that emphasized her desire to find an accurate diagnosis and her frustration at not "knowing what is wrong with me," despite having seen more than a dozen specialists. Dr Dordoni sympathized, "I know how you must feel . . . for me, not knowing is unbearable." Liz replied that before this consultation, "I was at the end of my rope with my trust in doctors and medicine." Lightly, the physician responded that she understood that she was now "under the gun" to rebuild Liz's trust.

Expanding on the reasons for the consultation, Liz explained that at Clinic A, she had been given a clinical diagnosis of hereditary ataxia, and she wanted it validated. The physician looked a bit puzzled.

Dr Dordoni:	Are you sure?
Liz:	No [I'm not sure], but that is what a doctor told me. At this point I'm not sure about anything anymore.
Dr Dordoni:	Have you had any genetic testing?
Liz:	[Obviously frustrated] I thought a test like that could give me a definitive answer but I wasn't offered it.
Dr Dordoni:	Who wouldn't be [frustrated] in your situation?

After completing the standard physical and cognitive evaluation, Dr Dordoni asked whether Liz had other concerns or questions. Liz quickly replied that since she "had been given the opportunity to be honest" she wanted to complain about the double message given by "this place [Clinic B]":

On the one hand, your clinic says this is "it" . . . the Mecca [laughs], where we would get the best care available. On the other, when you want to make an appointment . . . you're placed on a waiting list that may last for years.

Laughing a bit self-consciously, Dr Dordoni replied that now that Liz had "arrived at Mecca" the least they could do was to fulfill her expectations.

The doctor reviewed the list of Liz's medications and dosages, apologizing for asking her to repeat the information and adding with regard to her vitamin and mineral supplements that ". . . it could be an important piece of information to know as much as possible about your vitamin consumption because some forms of non-genetic ataxia can be caused by vitamin deficiencies." Liz appeared bored with this review until, referring to one particular drug, the doctor asked:

Dr Dordoni:	Did it make your hair fall out?
Liz:	No.
Dr Dordoni:	[laughingly] I'm kidding. Just checking . . . I wanted to know if you're paying attention . . . because this review is kind of boring . . . Right?

Both laughed and Liz volunteered that she has been experiencing a recent increase in the intensity of her hand tremors. Observing them and then taking Liz's hands, the physician commented,

Dr Dordoni:	What beautiful nail care! Who did it?
Liz:	A nail shop in [a nearby neighborhood].
Dr Dordoni:	You must give me the address. And don't think I'm not paying attention to your tremors. I'm doing my job; I am doing my job . . .
Liz:	I'm not worried. I see you're doing a good job.
Dr Dordoni:	Now I'll show my notes to my boss. We will review everything . . . and we'll be coming back soon . . . I don't want you to tell him I didn't pay attention to your tremors [laughs].
Liz:	Don't worry. I'll put in a good word for you.

Dr Dordoni left the examination room for 25 minutes, returning with Dr King, an attending physician. After a brief introduction, Dr King asked more questions about Liz's vitamin regimen. The interaction remained casual and relaxed, with medical topics interspersed with jokes and small talk. This general levity may have encouraged Paul, who until that point had been generally silent, and had been consistently silent during the consultation at Clinic A, to intervene. He once again voiced his fear that Liz might be vulnerable to the same rude and aggressive behavior they had seen in her father before he died. Listening attentively, Dr King replied:

> First, we don't expect she will get to that point and second, if you see any sign of that . . . we have wonderful resources to deal with that type of problem. I can refer you to a psychiatrist who is very well liked by patients and families . . . and to start, if you want, I can give you the name of our social worker who can help you a lot with the day-to-day management of the situation.

Turning his attention back to Liz, Dr King explained that he had reviewed Dr Dordoni's evaluation and the reports from Clinic A. Stating that although he held the specialists who evaluated Liz at Clinic A in the highest regard, he nevertheless felt that something was missing: "You are in good hands there [referring to specialists in Clinic A], it's an excellent clinic, but I feel there's a big gap in their evaluation." Dr King added that Liz's "clinical analysis would be enriched by a genetic diagnosis."

Liz enthusiastically agreed and began to tell him about her father's illness. Paul timidly added that they had also been concerned about the symptoms of Liz's brother, wondering whether they might be due to something that ran in the family. Dr King immediately offered to examine the brother and, although Liz had distanced herself from him, she volunteered to coordinate a consultation.

As the entire consultation drew to a close, Liz reported feeling better already because "the process" seemed to be moving along: "I wanted to do something but I felt trapped . . . Now I feel we are working on it . . . I was losing faith in medicine." Dr King enthusiastically responded:

> This is exactly the kind of talk I want to hear from my patients, and I'd like to concentrate with you on three things: one, to test you again to see how you metabolize your vitamins; second and more importantly, I will ask for a genetic test; and third, to do a more careful examination of your ear. I don't mean to say that your imbalance and tremors are due to hearing problems . . . but I am pretty sure that your symptoms could worsen if, for example, you are suffering from an acute form of vertigo . . . so these are all things we need to explore.

The four talked for a while longer about insurance matters, paperwork, scheduling, and finally, the signed consent forms for genetic testing. Dr King also asked Liz to bring all her previous test results on her return visit so they could analyze them in-depth toward developing a "good plan to get better." Clearly excited with a concrete plan for genetic testing, Liz offered, "Tell me where I have to sign and I will sign it now!" Sharing her sense of excitement, Dr King said that the forms would be ready momentarily and promised that "things will improve" if Liz followed the "to do" list they had developed together.

1 August

Meeting with Liz nearly a month after her neurogenetics evaluations at the two specialty clinics, we learned that she was still waiting for test results from both facilities. Nevertheless, her spirit remained high because she felt confident that Clinic B's doctors were "finally on the right track." We asked her to clarify, since it seemed that both clinics had taken similar approaches in asking for more time to conduct testing and analyze all of her clinical information. She elaborated that initially she had been completely satisfied with her experience at Clinic B and that the doctors there had restored her sense of hope. We then asked one of our standard interview questions, "Where on a scale of one to ten, with ten being the best, would you rate your consultation at Clinic B?" Without hesitating, she replied:

> [I would rate them a] ten! No question! They were extremely helpful with the paperwork. It was a lot of paperwork needed for the insurance – and [they were] very efficient. I hope to have the test results in a couple of weeks.

But all in all I have a more clear picture about the medication. Physical and speech therapy are also under way.

Asked whether there was anything else she took into account when assessing her experience at Clinic B, she added:

> The doctor [in charge] gave me the sense that something could be done, that for me, everything was not lost. I'm very sensitive about this [issue] because in the last year or so, when I was at a doctor's office and they said that they couldn't find what caused [my symptoms] . . . and I looked at my husband and I saw the disappointment in his face . . . I felt he was going to give up on me. This time [at Clinic B] they were very friendly, doctors, nurses . . . and they gave me something to work on and that's what I wanted. I know my condition is serious, I know it can't be fixed immediately . . . but at least they gave me hope . . . They pay attention when I talk. The doctor, the chief . . . seemed to be very well prepared . . . and he trusted me. Some doctors, in past years seemed skeptical [about level of my dedication] to my own care. They seemed to believe that I was missing doses of the medicines they prescribed . . . and I assure you that is not the case. I was careful [with the medicines] . . . I'm well organized, I'm an accountant, I know the value of organization. I know how to take care of things.

We then asked, "Anything else you want to add about your experience at Clinic B?" Liz replied:

> As I said, they seemed interested in helping me get to the bottom of things. One of the doctors [at Clinic B], when I said I felt frustrated by the lack of information I was getting [from my previous consultations] said, "I don't blame you. I would feel the same" and I appreciated that. I felt she understood my frustration.

Asked again about her experiences at Clinic A, Liz stated that while the doctors there were "nice," she felt as though she was not taken seriously by them:

> What made me mad, really mad . . . was that after waiting for a week, and them having my records in their office for so many days, they asked for more time to review my files. How could that be possible? I got the feeling that they didn't look at them until I came to see them.

3 October

A phone conversation with Liz revealed that all the tests at both clinics, including the genetic test at Clinic B, were "inconclusive." She had decided to continue treatment only at Clinic B where she was being offered a new vitamin regimen, along with physical and speech therapy. She reported feeling somewhat better although she was unable to recount any specific changes in her symptoms.

10 November

Liz's health continued to deteriorate despite her assiduous efforts with physical and speech therapy. Walking was becoming increasingly difficult and it had become harder for us to understand her speech. She also reported feeling deeply depressed and was thinking of requesting a psychiatric evaluation. She remained generally satisfied with her care at Clinic B but said she was losing faith in their ability to provide meaningful treatments. "It seems that the only thing I'm getting there is sympathy," she said.

The year ended without further efforts on our part to contact Liz. In January, we renewed our interest in seeing how she was doing. After trying without luck for several months, we finally reached her in June.

16 June

By phone, Liz sounded extremely sad, reporting she felt that her health was deteriorating more rapidly than last year. Although she remained satisfied with the relationships she had established at Clinic B, her hope for an accurate diagnosis and her trust in medicine was practically nil. We asked if she wanted to talk more about her situation and she agreed, turning her narrative back to her initial search for answers:

> All I hear are things that can be considered in one way or another. As days pass, you're feeling worse and worse. [So] you do what one is supposed to do: go to the doctor to see what is wrong with you. Then you get confused because you see different interpretations [of your symptoms]. There were even those who thought that what I explained wasn't entirely real; they seemed to believe that it was only in my mind. But I knew it was real. They thought I was depressed because I mentioned that many days I wondered if life was worth living. I don't know who is right and who is wrong. The only thing I know is that I lost my confidence in [medical] knowledge and I need to find my own way to cope with this. My husband is trying to help . . . but he can't.

Despite multiple efforts during the next several months, we were unable to reestablish contact with Liz. Since June, our calls were neither answered nor returned. Fearing we had lost contact entirely, we made one final attempt to communicate with her, see how she was doing, and extend our best wishes for her upcoming birthday.

31 October

Hearing our voice through her answering machine, Liz picked up the phone and explained that her speech had deteriorated to such an extent that she felt too self-conscious for phone conversations. After a brief chat, Liz thanked us for calling and we promised to call again in the New Year.

As had been the case in the past, in the months that followed we continued to find it difficult to reach either Liz or her husband by telephone.

12 February

On our tenth attempt since our last conversation at the end of October we were successful. Paul answered and told us that Liz's health had continued to deteriorate and
that she no longer used the telephone. He added that she wanted to stop attending
consultations at Clinic B, and altogether give up on medical care. In an effort to
keep her spirit up, Paul told us he had begun encouraging her to pursue alternative
medicine, but that so far, his attempts had been unsuccessful.

Analysis; hope and the limits of medical care

Society's desire to want to treat/cure vs. manage.

Liz had fervently hoped a genetic diagnosis would finally open the door to once and
for all launch her on a road toward healing. But in the end, genetic testing proved no
more helpful than any of her previous efforts. At her first stop, Clinic A, although
Liz did not explicitly *request* genetic testing, privately, while we were waiting for
her specialty consultation to begin, she told us that she expected that she would be
offered a genetic test for two reasons: she had already been tentatively diagnosed
with a hereditary ataxia and she had been referred to a genetics specialty clinic. She
herself thought a genetic diagnosis was a plausible route to pursue since both her
father and her only brother seemed to have similar symptoms. But to her surprise
and disappointment, Clinic A's neurogenetics specialists felt that her symptoms
were not consistent with any known condition that could be detected through
genetic testing, and accordingly, never offered her a genetic test. Clinic B's neurogenetics specialists, on the other hand, were entirely willing to pursue genetic testing but alas, that test failed to conclusively show a genetic cause for her symptoms
and the information did not move her doctors any closer to a definitive diagnosis.

   Still, even as her health continued to deteriorate, Liz convinced herself that if
only she could get an accurate ("precise") diagnosis, she would begin moving
toward better health. Indeed, diagnosis – the corralling and categorizing of an
unruly set of symptoms – is the first step toward healing. In Kathryn Montgomery's
words, "To know the cause of disease is to have control" (Montgomery 2006: 57).
Liz's need for an accurate diagnosis may have been especially strong in light of her
professional training with numbers, the most "precise" of organizing rubrics, and
the very rational approach to problem solving that forms the basis for working with
them. During our first meeting, Liz told us she no longer knew who she was and
thereafter, often reflected ruefully on her increasing inability to keep track of numbers, which had forced her to abandon her profession. Even more threatening to her
core identity was the progressive loss of her ability to make financial decisions,
which had brought the couple to the brink of bankruptcy, and, in Liz's view, had
nearly destroyed her marriage.

   During the time we knew her (and even beforehand), Liz's medical experiences
could be compared to a roller coaster ride: she approached each new clinician with
a renewed sense of hope – only to be let down time after time, or as she put it "coming up empty handed." Her expectations of Clinic B, her "Mecca," were especially
high, possibly because it had been so hard to get an appointment, but also because

she had heard that the doctors there had outstanding reputations. They had also offered something completely new: a genetic test that promised to confirm that her elusive symptoms were not fabricated, as previous physicians had implied, but were in fact inherited from her father. This explanation would be doubly satisfying since, as she noted, he "never passed on anything of value to us [kids], anyway."

Liz's exceptional determination to get to "the bottom of things" set her apart from her father and her brother, who, in her eyes, had passively awaited their destiny without fighting back. Conversely, Liz was willing to invest all the time, money, and energy she could into her search for a diagnosis and effective treatment because she was sure she would eventually get answers. Somehow, she never allowed herself to consider that it could be otherwise. Unfortunately, instead of answers, Liz received only intensified and more rapidly progressing symptoms. Yet, despite all of her previous experiences, our final conversations revealed that she remained "satisfied" with the medical care at Clinic B even though her "trust" in the clinic's doctors and her hopeful belief that they could help had evaporated.

In the course of telling Liz's story, we have used the terms *satisfaction*, *trust*, and *hope*. At this juncture, some definitions are in order. In medical relationships – like others of inherent inequality – trust on the part of the more vulnerable agent entails delegating power to another person with the expectation that the other will care for and make efforts to help (Grimen 2008; Hall, Dugan, and Mishra 2001). Living with the debilitating symptoms and uncertainties of neurodegenerative disease is a quintessential example of this kind of vulnerability. Although some argue that greater vulnerability on the part of patients can lead to greater trust (Katz 1984), Liz's experience may be more accurately described as a situation where physicians appear to have been imbued with demigod characteristics. For Liz, as well as for many others in our study, greater vulnerability assuredly did not evoke greater trust in clinicians.

In Liz's case, we must also differentiate between a trusting *attitude* and trusting *behavior*. Following Liz's story we can infer that although her attitude toward medicine was progressively becoming more distrustful, particularly after several ultimately disappointing visits to Clinic A, her decision to continue her quest for an accurate diagnosis at Clinic B showed that she nonetheless maintained trusting behavior.

Shifting her care from Clinic A to Clinic B gave Liz the opportunity to reestablish some of her previously-eroded trust in the medical system. She liked the staff at Clinic B's casual, friendly, and helpful style of interaction, the sense that she was being heard, and the feelings of sympathy they offered. But even more meaningful was the fact that the staff at Clinic B restored her sense of hope that a different approach could lead to an unambiguous diagnosis and the abatement of her symptoms.

Analyzing Liz's experiences led us to reflect upon the relationship between trust and satisfaction in the context of medical care. While related, they refer to separate processes: satisfaction is used in the context of evaluating performance, in other words, past behaviors, whereas trust is about future expectations (Murphy and Holmes 1997). During our last conversation, we saw that this distinction remained

importance of patient – clinician. R\n
gets satisfaction

clear in Liz's mind. Although she had decided to stop seeing the doctors at Clinic B, she told us that she was still satisfied with the care she had received there. However, with the genetic test having failed to provide an answer, she lost trust in the ability of the clinic's doctors to help her and, by extension, in the diagnostic and curative power of biomedicine. It was Paul, however, who reintroduced the possibility that hope could be restored through a new approach – alternative medicine, a vast domain of seemingly infinite possibilities.

Liz's story casts grim light on some of the more demoralizing aspects of living with neurodegenerative disease. Not all of the patients in our study were as preoccupied with the need for an accurate diagnosis as was Liz. This quest gave her life a sense of purpose when she could no longer act in ways that had previously provided meaning and coherence. Although the last bastion of hope seemed to crumble when she came to realize that her "Mecca" offered no new answers, Paul stepped in to pick up the mantle, striving to reinvigorate Liz's sense of hope.

In Chapter 2 we will continue to explore the contexts in which patients who are chronically ill – and as a consequence, emotionally vulnerable – may develop and sustain feelings of hope. Unlike Liz, Ana, whom we meet in the next case study, eventually did get an accurate genetic diagnosis, something she had tirelessly searched for over the course of many years. But the genetic information failed to provide the kinds of answers Ana was seeking and, like Liz, Ana's ability to continue to deploy hopeful feelings about the future was jeopardized as well.

2 Destination unknown

When patients fall ill, they sometimes feel they lack the vocabulary to adequately communicate their subjective sense of suffering. The questions doctors ask in their efforts to get to the bottom of the problem may reveal a yawning gap between patients' embodied experience and physicians' conceptions of the meaning of a set of signs and symptoms. Doctors, too, say they are frequently frustrated by the complexities associated with communicating medical information to lay patients and the imprecise descriptions patients often give them as to the nature of their distress. Physician and medical anthropologist Arthur Kleinman reports that doctors often find patients' accounts of what is troubling them characterized by "vagueness, multiplicity of meanings, frequent changes and lack of sharp boundaries between ideas and experiences" (Kleinman 1980:107). All of this can make it difficult for doctors to rely much on patients' conceptualizations and explanations as they go about seeking to discover the causes, contexts, and precise manifestations of their patients' suffering. Social analysts have therefore found it productive to analytically distinguish between "illness" – patients' subjective experiences and personal interpretations, and "disease" – objectively identifiable clusters of abnormalities organized into discrete categories that provide the scientific basis for diagnosis, prognosis, and treatment (Hahn and Kleinman 1983; Helman 1985). But these neat distinctions easily lose meaning when applied to many of the neurodegenerative movement disorder patients in our study. As we will show throughout this monograph, patients sought to understand the cause of vague and variable symptoms of long duration that often not only failed to conform to a clear pattern for diagnosis, but also did not respond to any known treatment.

We saw this clearly with Liz Morgan in Chapter 1. Over the years we knew her, she never received a meaningful diagnosis, even as her symptoms steadily worsened. Sadly, her experience was not unique. Many others in our study endured similar trajectories. And to make things worse, the longer their symptoms resisted diagnosis, the more likely their reality would be questioned by clinicians and family members – even to the point of labeling them "crazy" or "overly sensitive," as Liz told us, and as we will see when we meet Ana Almendra. As did Ana, some even begin to question their own experience and wonder whether they are, in fact, mentally unbalanced, inventing, or somehow causing their own symptoms. These demoralizing experiences are, of course, not limited to patients with neurodegenerative disease. In their brilliant analysis of the nature of classification, Geoffrey C. Bowker and Susan Leigh Star refer to this phenomenon as "the separation of the patient from ownership of their condition" (Bowker and Starr 1999: 84; see also Bharadwaj, Atkinson, and Clarke 2006).

Ana's story also shows how communication between doctors and patients with chronic, vague, and difficult to diagnose symptoms may fail if the two have different temporal orientations and/or expectations regarding the disease process. Although doctors practice medicine within what philosopher Kay Toombs has termed a spatial or a-temporal frame, patients inevitably experience their disease unfolding in real time (Toombs 1990). Moreover, with regard to the significance of temporality in the experience of illness, Ana's story also illuminates what may happen when a sensitive child grows up in a family with a chronically ill parent. We show that the meaning Ana gave to her somatic experiences as a child and her fears about her future were filtered through the lens of her father's medical problems.

Ana's narrative simultaneously illustrates the experiences of two types of patients: those who were actively "searching for answers" in order to understand and, if possible, find things they could do to more effectively control the downward progression of their symptoms, and those who actually had a diagnosis, whether or not from genetic testing, despite the fact that this diagnosis might not necessarily be considered totally accurate by the patient. Ana's case, moreover, offers a poignant example of the types of difficulties that can ensue when patients and clinicians employ divergent explanatory paradigms to interpret the significance of a set of symptoms.

Background

We were introduced to Ana Almendra, a 37-year-old divorced mother of two young children, in the waiting room of one of our participating specialty clinics. Ana had been referred by her new general neurologist and was accompanied by Robert, her ex-husband. She held a high-level administrative position in a private company that serviced the entertainment industry and he worked in maintenance for a state agency. Just ten days earlier, Ana learned that the genetic test she had taken for Huntington's disease (H.D.) had come back positive, which meant that over time she would almost certainly come down with the disease. Given the gravity of this finding and her insatiable appetite for medical information, her general neurologist felt a consultation with a neurogenetics specialist could be helpful. Ana was acutely interested in learning more about her prognosis and treatment options, particularly the availability of drugs to delay the onset of disabling Huntington's symptoms.

Huntington's disease, formerly known as Huntington's Chorea, is an incurable, progressive, and ultimately fatal brain disorder. It is caused by a "repeat expansion" of a single gene, which means the gene contains too many copies of one of its sequences of nucleotides. Chorea refers to the jerky involuntary movements that are the disease's most prominent symptom and were the main basis for diagnosis before the advent of linkage testing for H.D. in 1986. Other common symptoms include mild tremor, clumsiness, and difficulties concentrating and remembering things; mood changes including depression; and in some cases, aggressive behavior. Children born to a parent with the Huntington gene have a 50 percent chance of inheriting the disease. Age of onset is typically between 40 and 50, although symptoms may begin to appear in childhood or adolescence. While early symptoms may vary, eventually most cognitive and motor functions are affected, and in its later stages, patients lose their ability to control bodily functions. Death is caused not by Huntington's disease per se, but by associated complications, the most common of which are pneumonia, heart failure, choking, and malnutrition.

Between April 2004 and May 2005, we had 16 encounters with Ana, including face-to-face meetings, phone calls, and sporadic chats during church visits. Analyzing Ana's narrative accounts was particularly challenging due to her tendency to fuse her present, past, and imagined future experiences into a single story, using each to help define and inform the rest. Although we generally tried to keep our conversations focused on her current health and medical care issues and experiences, she often responded to our questions by saying, "[I'll tell you] . . . but let me first put things in order." This process usually involved drawing on memories, experiences, and feelings from adolescence and childhood.

At the time of our first meeting, Ana was coming to terms with the fact that her genetic test showed that she carried the Huntington gene – news that was for her at once devastating, validating, and strangely liberating. It marked the culmination of a 14-year quest to discover the cause of persistent symptoms she had suffered since adolescence, and validation of her belief that she had in fact inherited her symptoms from her father.

As a teenager, Ana had tried to simply "tough it out," but she explained, "As I got older, the need to know the truth became almost an obsession." She reached a turning point in her early twenties when Ana saw her father for the first time in more than ten years. She explained, "Getting the disease was on my mind from the moment I saw my father in 1990. I had remembered him as a big, handsome man and when I saw him, I couldn't believe it, he was a bag of bones. . . ." Because Ana had since become the mother of two young children, she felt further impelled to face the possibility that she, too, might have the same disease and she wanted to plan for their future while she was still able. These uncertainties were foremost in Ana's mind during the neurology consultation where we first met.

Growing up in a working-class family (her mother worked part time as a cashier; her father was on disability), Ana told us that for as long as she could remember, she "felt" different from others her own age, as well as from her only sibling, Susana, who was two years older. During grade school, she thought she and Susana were the only kids being raised by a single mother. She never knew whether her father had left of his own accord or if her mother had kicked him out. Although she could count on her father to take her side in her frequent fights with Susana, she also recalled him to be "a terrible person – short tempered, rude and aggressive." She particularly remembered his unpredictable mood swings and her parents' frequent loud arguments, until the day he simply vanished from her life at age ten. Over time, Ana came to believe that H.D. was "the bullet that had destroyed [her] family." She said she never felt "whole" again after he had left; "It may be because of that, that I wanted so bad to have my own family." His leaving also meant that Ana lost her only dependable ally in her fights with Susana, "Life became hell for me because my mother and sister were always together and I always felt outside."

As a teenager, Ana's unhappiness persisted. She found it hard to make friends and felt awkward and clumsy. Frequent, inexplicable mood changes made her think she might have inherited her father's "personality." She would become frightened when older relatives remarked that she took after him – although in retrospect, she thinks they were only referring to the brown hair and eyes they shared. At the time, though, she hated to hear them talk that way because the last thing she wanted was to be like him. Even harder to bear than her own mood swings was her mother's carping, "You're just like your father," because deep down, she feared it might be so.

Ana believed that her own feelings of inadequacy and her inability "to connect" contributed to her experience of chronic depression for which she began to seek treatment in late adolescence. Although, at the time, she considered herself "a difficult person to be around," she came to believe that all her problems were due to "something" she had inherited from her father and she continued to resent her family's unwillingness to recognize that she was ill. "They preferred to believe it was all in my head," she explained. She attributed her ability to have maintained her "sanity" during those long dark years and her strength to continue her search for a diagnosis to her strong religious faith.

Ana finally sought genetic testing after being moved by a terrifying story about a Huntington family on Dateline TV. She explained, "I got so scared. There was this person with H.D.; he became extremely nervous, like I am now, and all of a sudden he was so paranoid that he killed his family!" Since the time she saw her father in the hospital dying and she learned the cause of his disease, she had been consumed with the worry that she might somehow have the same thing. But the show steeled her determination to finally learn "with security" what to expect, if indeed, Huntington's was to be her fate. Recently divorced and increasingly worried about her children's future, she became convinced that she should not wait any longer. Aware of Ana's overpowering fear that she was already ill with H.D., her psychotherapist encouraged her to pursue genetic testing in the hope that the test would be negative and that such a finding would relieve her anxieties. Her mother, who had earlier been opposed to Ana's pursuit of genetic testing, reluctantly and somewhat ambivalently, gave her support. Ana recounted, "When I told her I was going to get the test she said a couple of strong words that are burned in my mind." Switching to Spanish, she continued, *¡Ana, no debes remover la mierda si no quieres oler a podrido!* ("Ana, you shouldn't move the shit if you don't want to smell rotten!").

While the positive test result was devastating, Ana nevertheless found it useful because it meant she must begin planning and perhaps, even more importantly, because it validated her long-held conviction that she was not just "making it up."

Mapping the way to an uncertain destination

Although Ana's long road to a meaningful diagnosis began when she was still in her twenties, until she tested positive for the Huntington's gene her doctors and relatives had considered her physically healthy, but somewhat unbalanced mentally. Ana, however, was certain her problems were not psychogenic and, for a time, thought they might have been caused by teenage drug experimentation. Far more troubling was the nagging fear that they were somehow linked to "the phantasm of [her] father." But neither of these explanations persuaded her clinicians, especially the neurology specialists she consulted. This may in part have been because the uncontrolled movements she sometimes experienced never occurred during medical consultations and the doctors did not seem to understand her descriptions of them (she called them "sensations"). As a result, the standard referral was to a mental health professional. It is also possible that Ana herself was not ready to face the accurate diagnosis she said she was seeking.

As we will see, however, the positive genetic test did not mark the end of Ana's journey. Despite the test results, her neurogenetics specialty clinicians remained unconvinced that the involuntary movements, mood swings, and memory problems Ana reported were, in fact, early H.D. symptoms; these doctors considered Ana "asymptomatic" for H.D. For Ana, this was an agonizing repetition of the old pattern. Even with the genetic test results finally in hand, Ana's experience of illness and her doctors' assessment of her disease once again failed to converge! Accordingly – and understandably – Ana's frustration with clinicians and with family members who failed to recognize her "sensations" as real symptoms permeated every one of our conversations.

Because our larger purpose is to cast light on the process of searching for a diagnosis and treatment for symptoms that are variable, vague, and resist disease classification, we analyzed and tied together scattered fragments from our many formal and informal conversations with Ana towards tracking when and why clinicians agreed with her explanations – and when, and if possible, why they did not.

Fourteen years earlier

Ana was surprised to get a call from a county hospital telling her that her father was dying. Recently married, she and her new husband, Robert, had rushed to the hospital, where they learned that her father had been clinically diagnosed with H.D. (genetic testing was not yet available). It had been years since they had had any contact, and she was overcome with emotion when she learned that, at age 50, he had been homeless for several years. At the hospital, she was also surprised to learn that other close relatives on her father's side, including an aunt, seemed to have experienced neurological problems, but a "lack of information" prevented her father's doctors from determining whether his relatives could also have been suffering from H.D.

While visiting her father in the hospital, Ana told us she briefly spoke with the doctor in charge who Ana remembers as a general practitioner we call Dr One. Ana asked her whether she thought that Ana, her sister, and even her future children could have the same thing as her father, explaining that she had long had "sensations" that could be viewed as similar to her father's symptoms. She added that she referred to them as "sensations" because they were not easy to see, consistent, or predictable. She elaborated that they usually consisted of muscle pain in her extremities; spurts of immobility lasting a few seconds at a time; sometimes feeling a delay between when she thought about moving an extremity and her actual ability to do so; and a feeling of "being mad at the world," that is, a propensity toward irritability without apparent cause. It was this latter sensation she most feared. Pointblank, Ana asked Dr One whether she might have inherited her father's disease. Dr One advised Ana to see a neurologist to "evaluate [her] situation and perform the necessary tests" to determine if she was experiencing early symptoms of H.D.

We classified Dr One, a general practitioner's assessment of Ana's concerns, as congruent with her own because she reinforced the possibility that Ana's sensations could be a foreshadowing of H.D. symptoms and referred her to a neurology specialist to get a better understanding of her situation.

Ana's father died shortly after they were reunited. In the wake of his death, Ana spoke several times with her sister, Susana, about the benefit of being evaluated so that they would "be prepared" if necessary. Susana said she was not interested and tried to convince Ana not to pursue the subject any further either; their mother agreed. As Ana explained, "I was always in favor of knowing as much as we can . . . but my mom and my sister are those kind of people who prefer to hide things in order to keep up appearances."

Ana disregarded their advice and visited her own family doctor, whom we call Dr Two. Dr Two agreed with Dr One that Ana's sensations could be early signs of H.D. and offered to refer her to a neurologist. At first, Ana intended to pursue the referral, but either because of fear or as a result of her mother's and sister's resistance (or both), she did not, telling herself that she could live with her sensations and that her family could be right that they were mostly in her head.

We classified Dr Two, also a general practitioner's assessment, as congruent with Ana's. He agreed that her "sensations" could be a precursor to Huntington's symptoms and offered to provide a neurological referral.

Eleven years earlier

For the most part, Ana was in good health during these years. She gave birth to her daughter and was reveling in motherhood. The sensations continued but she said they were tolerable and that her main health problem was that she had gained weight during her pregnancy. She was preoccupied primarily with rocky family relations: her marriage was in serious trouble and she felt even more distant from her mother and sister. Ana had two psychological episodes during this time and sought help from two different psychiatrists. She was suffering deep depression and experienced frequent mood changes that included "explosions of anger." For two years she took medication to treat these symptoms but the side effects, which included difficulties concentrating, created problems at work and she abandoned the treatments.

Ana told both psychiatrists about her fears of having inherited H.D. and her belief that her sensations indicated the need for further evaluation. The first,

Dr Three, said that although he could not see a strong connection between Ana's "sensations" and her father's symptoms he thought it could be beneficial if she were to see a neurologist for an accurate diagnosis. The second, Dr Four, seems to have substantially disregarded Ana's views by merely making a recommendation for a new antidepressant, without making a neurology referral.

We classified the psychiatrist, Dr Three's perspective, as somewhat congruent with Ana's. While he said he did not believe that the "sensations" she was reporting had the same cause as her father's symptoms, he nevertheless suggested that she see a neurologist. We classified Dr Four's approach as non-congruent because he disregarded Ana's reports describing her symptoms and did not refer her for further neurological evaluation.

While Ana was in treatment with Dr Four, she followed Dr Three's advice and decided to consult with a neurologist. After the evaluation, Dr Five, a neurologist recommended by Ana's mother, reported that she "couldn't see anything wrong through the physical and cognitive evaluation" and concluded that Ana's symptoms could be the result of stress. She advised Ana to remain in psychiatric treatment and to start seeing a psychologist.

We classified Dr Five, a neurologist's perspective, as incongruent with Ana's since she suggested psychiatric treatment and additional psychotherapy rather than further neurological evaluation.

Nine years earlier

Following the advice of Dr Five, and also due to the turmoil in her life, Ana continued psychological treatment for the next two years. Dr Six, her psychologist at the time, focused mostly on her family problems, particularly her relationships with her husband and her sister (her relationship with her mother had started to improve). But Ana also talked at length with Dr Six about her fears of having possibly inherited H.D. and what the consequences might be for her daughter. This was also the first time Ana told any clinician about her early experiences with illicit substances, rationalizing them as "part of my rebellion phase" and that she "only [used them] for a short period of time."

Dr Six agreed with Dr Four that the symptoms she described, which at this time also included lack of coordination and a marked change in her handwriting, could be the result of uncontrolled anxiety.

We classified the perspective of Dr Six, a psychologist, as incongruent with Ana's since he concluded that her symptoms were due to anxiety.

Seven years earlier

Ana visited at least two more general practitioners and one specialist for persistent headaches, high blood pressure, and weight control. During those consultations she did not raise her concerns about H.D., although the "sensations" continued. She also discontinued psychotherapy.

Two years earlier

Ana began psychotherapy again. With Dr Seven, her new psychologist, she explored her fears about "not being able to care for [her] children if [she] ends up like [her] father." She and her husband were recently divorced, having had their second child, a son, two years earlier. Although she sought medical care for various ongoing problems, for the most part her doctors sought to reassure her that she was generally in good health. Ana herself was not convinced and revealed new concerns about being affected with H.D. after experiencing a fall. She had lost her balance on her way to work and said that, at the time, she wondered whether it was simply an accident or if it was due to H.D. She recounted thinking ominously as she was falling, "Oh my god! This is how it's going to be from now on . . .."

Dr Seven suggested that Ana see her family doctor to evaluate the episode and encouraged her to discuss her family medical history and her "sensations." Dr Eight, her new general practitioner, concluded that Ana's concerns warranted a neurological referral.

We classified the perspectives of Dr Seven, a psychologist, and Dr Eight, a general practitioner, as congruent with Ana's since they were receptive to her wish to pursue a medical diagnosis.

One year earlier

Ana consulted with Dr Seven, her psychologist, and Dr Eight, her GP, several more times. Based on her family history and continued efforts to draw their attention to the significance of her "sensations," Dr Eight supported Ana in her interest in genetic testing and authorized a referral to a neurologist, Dr Nine. After Dr Nine's clinical evaluation, he told her that he "wouldn't be against" genetic testing and suggested she begin by determining whether her insurance would pay for it. Her insurance carrier required a more detailed neurological assessment, at which point Dr Nine told Ana that he could not clinically justify genetic testing for H.D., but that if she were "really determined," she could ask for a letter from her psychologist, Dr Seven, to justify genetic testing for anxiety and deep depression. Ana was furious with Dr Nine's lack of understanding but nevertheless followed his advice and got the letter from Dr Seven. Soon afterwards, the insurance company authorized Ana's genetic test.

We classified Dr Nine, a neurologist's perspective, to be somewhat congruent with Ana's search because he supported her interest in genetic testing even though he did not help get the test paid for by her insurance carrier.

The present

Immediately upon learning that she had been approved for genetic testing, Ana decided to end her relationship with Dr Nine and found a new neurologist, Dr Ten. She was clear about her objectives when she booked her first appointment, telling the receptionist she wanted "to see the doctor to have an H.D. test." Dr Ten did a brief neurological evaluation that focused mostly on her medical history and current cognitive capabilities. He concluded that Ana's physical symptoms were inconclusive for H.D., but that based on her family history and high level of anxiety, the test would be beneficial.

Ana's worst fears were realized when the genetic test came back positive. Her extreme need for medical information about her prognosis moved Dr Ten to advise her to consult with a neurogenetics specialist, who could provide general information and more specific details regarding her prognosis and treatment options. She was following up on that recommendation when she came to the clinic where we met. There, two neurologists, who would be number eleven and twelve evaluated her: Dr Oaks, a fellow, and Dr King, the attending physician, the same doctor who treated Liz Morgan in Chapter 1.

During the consultation, Dr Oaks began by asking the reason for Ana's visit. Ana replied that now that she had a positive Huntington's gene test, she wanted to know when she would become disabled and unable to continue working. More important, she added, was her interest in any new drugs that might delay an advance in the severity of her symptoms ("sensations"). Dr Oaks proceeded to take Ana's medical history and then conducted a physical assessment, including standard movement, balance, and cognitive tests. She next said she wanted to discuss the possibility that Ana resume antidepressants with her supervisor, an idea that Ana was not very receptive to because of her previous experience of strong side effects.

Dr Oaks left and returned after about 45 minutes accompanied by Dr King, who apologized for the delay and then explained that he and Dr Oaks had "very carefully" reviewed all of Ana's information and "agreed on [their] assessment." He continued:

Dr King: First, we are in agreement that you are H.D. pre-symptomatic and that your symptoms may be from anxiety attacks and depression. I also agree with Dr Oaks's recommendation for antidepressants. There is no need to go through life feeling so anxious and fearful and sad when we have medication to help.

Ana: Doctor, I don't want that type of medication, well, it's not that I don't want it, it's that it makes me feel worse.

Dr King: How about taking half the dose and seeing if you feel better. If you don't, call me and we'll see if we can find something else that works better for you. Our goal is to find the exact doses for *you* . . . How about that?

Ana: [silence]

Dr King: Do you agree?

Ana: If you say so. [laughter]

Dr King: I like to hear you laughing. There is no need to feel fear. We are here with you all the way.

The doctor then asked Ana to walk across the examining room, then examined her hands and gave her a pen in order to observe her grasp, all the while commenting,

"Fine, fine," then continued, "I see you are fine. We will do our best to keep you well."

Ana: Thanks, doctor. [pause] I don't want to end up like my father.
Dr King: You won't. You're an entirely and totally different person. Genetically, sure, you got something from him. [laughs] But you also got something from your mother and it seems to me that the stuff you got from your mother is good. See? You have the positive H.D. test. But you don't have symptoms of H.D. yet. That's good. I know you think you do but if they are, I'll tell you they are very, very mild. So your mother's genes, which seem to be okay, are defending your body from those other genes that are repeating and repeating.

Dr King told her that while involuntary movements are one of the most common characteristics of Huntington's, Ana's did not fit the H.D. pattern and that while her mood changes, memory loss, writing, and balance problems were, in fact, all common manifestations of the disease, their evaluations showed hers to be within normal range. Ana was not persuaded. She repeated that she didn't want to "end up just like my father. My mother says that my father began to show symptoms when he was in his thirties and now that I am in my late thirties, that is happening to me too!"

The physicians continued to paint a more hopeful picture. Dr King volunteered that the experience of Huntington's patients was actually quite variable and that they expected that Ana's disease would advance slowly because her genetic test showed she carried "just" 43 repeats of the defective nucleotide sequence and that this was considered "in the middle range with regard to when symptoms usually begin."[1] Moreover, Ana did not drink alcohol like her father did, her maternal genes seemed very healthy, and her overall health and lifestyle were very good, all to her advantage. Ana remained tearful, traumatized, and skeptical: "I *know* that my symptoms are from Huntington's. I know that – and I don't want to end up like him!"

We classified the perspectives of Dr Oaks and Dr King as non-congruent with Ana's because they regarded her as asymptomatic for H.D. while she was certain they were wrong.

Colliding paradigms: patient and doctor, illness and disease

One of Ana's main motivations, in her words, "almost an obsession" from the time she was reunited with her father and learned that he was dying from the complications of an inherited disease to the present, was to "discover the truth" about the cause of the social, emotional and physical problems she had suffered for as long as she could remember. She found herself repeatedly thwarted by relatives who "preferred not to know" and physicians, too many of whom offered psychiatric based explanations.

When we analyzed the extent of congruence between Ana and the 12 doctors she consulted, we see there was agreement between just four: Dr One, Dr Two, Dr Seven, and Dr Eight (three general practitioners and a psychologist). Dr Four, Dr Five, Dr Six, Dr Oaks, and Dr King (three neurologists, one psychiatrist, and one psychologist) did not share Ana's view that her "sensations" were early H.D. "symptoms" and instead attributed her problems to depression, anxiety, or other mental problems. Dr Three, Dr Nine, and Dr Ten (two neurologists and a psychiatrist) were somewhat neutral, with Three and Ten appearing to be inclined toward validating Ana's experience. Dr Nine was willing to entertain the possibility that Ana's symptoms might be caused by H.D., but was not willing to make that case with her insurance carrier. Dr Ten regarded her symptoms as "inconclusive" for H.D., but was nevertheless willing to order a genetic test.

In summarizing the perspectives of these dozen clinicians Ana consulted during her long quest for answers to legitimate her experience and prove she was not somatizing her anxiety, we discern the following pattern:

The three general practitioners were consistent in their views. All appeared receptive to the possibility that a neurodegenerative process might have caused the somatic experiences she reported and they validated Ana's need to discover a physical cause for her distress. Their approach to diagnosis appeared to reflect what they had been taught: when a patient with a family history of Huntington's disease presents vague neurological symptoms, a referral to a neurologist is the first course of action.

The four mental health professionals showed the greatest heterogeneity in their responses, and we could detect no obvious pattern beyond the fact that they appeared more inclined toward a psychological than a physical explanation for Ana's problems, which is not altogether surprising.

More interesting to us, and infuriating to Ana, were the neurologists who, while-formally trained in diagnosing the type of condition Ana believed was affecting her, most consistently failed to provide the clarity she sought. Of greatest disappointment was that even with medicine's most compelling evidence in hand, an objective test demonstrating she had indeed inherited the Huntington gene, the neurogenetics experts still would not legitimate her belief that her somatic manifestations were early symptoms of H.D. Instead, they still considered her a disease-free person who would eventually become ill, but whose present problems were mainly psychological in origin.

What accounted for this marked diversity of medical responses? In all instances, Ana offered the same set of ambiguous symptoms; symptoms that on their face could be construed as consistent with Huntington's disease. Insight might be found in Jerome Groopman's recent commentary on contemporary medical practices in which he shows that doctors often base medical decisions on intuition rather than deliberate analysis or empirical findings. As he puts it, "Hypotheses about [a] diagnosis come to a doctor's mind even before a word of the medical history is spoken" (Groopman 2007:12). But while that first intense flash of knowing can often prove absolutely correct in the long run, jumping too quickly to a conclusion can cause one to disregard or dismiss critical information that does not fit into the expected pattern, as we saw in Ana's case. Groopman's findings also help to explain why Ana's experience with doctors was so painfully variable.

We also found that in her quest for a diagnosis, Ana and her clinicians, particularly the neurogenetics specialists, were moving through divergent spatial and temporal dimensions. This is because any illness, particularly one that is chronic, can disrupt our perception of life's linear continuity (Ablon 1995; Becker 1980; Kaufman 1988; Scheer and Luborsky 1991). Ana's story offers a poignant example of this. The meaning of her "sensations" was informed by terrifying memories of her father on his deathbed and the fears of an identical fate in her own imagined future, in addition to rather than purely as the result of her actual current experience. For this reason, her chance stumble and increasing writing difficulties evoked palpable terror that the downward H.D. spiral had already begun.

Others born into families that carry the Huntington gene have written moving personal accounts documenting the singular nature of their travail: Sue Wright describes the "yo-yo type of existence" she endured during many years when she was undecided about whether to be tested (Wright 1996: 5–7); Julia Madigan communicates the welter of contradictory emotions she experienced after her negative test result: "I felt wonderful for a little while and then after some time I felt terrible" (Madigan 1996: 7–22); an anonymous author defiantly defends her decision not to be tested (Anonymous 1996: 23–26) (see also Etchegory 2006; Konrad 2005; Wexler 1996).

In Ana's case, the long road to discovery might have been considerably shortened had her own ideas about the cause of her "sensations" been taken more seriously earlier on. Ana's personal quest began in 1993, the very year the Huntington's gene was found. Had she gotten different responses from her clinicians, Ana's identity as a legitimate patient, albeit an "asymptomatic" one, might also have been achieved far sooner. But whether knowing her genetic status when she was much younger would have been more a benefit than a burden remains unknown: Ana told us that if she had the option of genetic testing at the beginning, she might never have fulfilled her dreams of becoming a mother and having a "normal" family.

Genetic testing enables clinicians to make certain diagnoses much earlier than if they are relying solely on clinical findings because the latter means a disease process is already manifesting. As the genetic bases for disease become better understood than they are today, more of us will be given genetic diagnoses and told we are "asymptomatic" or "pre-symptomatic" patients (Hess, Preloran, and Browner 2009; Konrad 2003). As just shown, there will be both benefits and burdens. Some will be motivated to adopt what they believe to be healthier behaviors and lifestyles to try to slow or avert the disease process. Others, like Ana, may become fatalistic or sufficiently preoccupied with the knowledge to evoke negative consequences for their mental and physical health. Thus, a positive genetic test in the absence of medically recognized symptoms can have paradoxical effects: as in Ana's case, such a diagnosis can validate subjective experience. But it can also retroactively and retrospectively expand the temporal perception and trajectory of an illness. Some bioethicists and other social commentators are also concerned that as the genetic bases of more conditions are identified, employers, insurance carriers, and even the government will assume even greater health monitoring functions. In such a scenario, Ana might well have been pressured not to have her own biological children because of the risk of their inheriting the Huntington gene; the very children who today inspire her to try to stay healthy and to continue to actively pursue appropriate treatments.

Part II

Coming to terms with devastating prognoses

In Part I we considered two patients' quests to discover the cause of their symptoms, and the meanings they gave to the actual and potential medical explanations, genetic and otherwise, that they gathered along the way. Part II explores how patients may deal with diagnostic explanations derived from genetic testing over the long term.

We offer analyses of the paths taken by two patients in their determination to discover the cause of their symptoms. Each held hope that a genetic explanation for their rapidly deteriorating health would at the very least provide the peace of mind of knowing what the future held in store and the opportunity to plan accordingly. Most of the other study participants similarly believed that a genetic diagnosis would provide information that would allow them to better cope with their increasingly circumscribed daily existences: nearly two-thirds of patients and over half of family members gave as their chief reasons for seeking medical attention either a more precise diagnosis or better information about their prognosis, and in this context would welcome a genetic – or indeed, any – diagnosis.

In Chapter 3, we meet Enrique Silvestre who, when he learned that his gait and balance problems were due to having inherited the gene for Friedreich's ataxia, responded with the "can do" spirit he had evidently brought to every challenge he had previously faced. The gravity of his prognosis led him to conclude that his quality of life would be much better back in his home country, and even as his genetic diagnosis forced him to reevaluate some of his core beliefs about identity, family, and destiny, he immediately set out to carefully plan all of the details for a new life.

Carlos Estrada and some of his close relatives offer their narrative accounts in Chapter 4. Carlos and his two sisters were afflicted with Spinal Muscular Atrophy (SMA), a motor neuron disorder caused by a defective gene. We see how the illness manifested with different levels of intensity in the three siblings and with differing effects on their day-to-day activities. Carlos became deeply depressed upon learning that a genetic test confirmed that his condition was both inherited and incurable. But as time went on, his mood brightened as he began to envision a new life back in Mexico that would allow him to hold on to his cherished position as head of his family, despite his worsening symptoms.

The lives of Enrique Silvestre, Carlos Estrada, and others in our study were transformed when they learned that their conditions were, in fact, genetic. Having a specific diagnosis assuaged uncertainties they had struggled with for many years. And finally knowing what would be in store motivated them to create complex strategies for confronting the progressive consequences of their devastating diseases. Together, the chapters explore some of the issues of identity, self-worth, and independence experienced by individuals suffering from genetically caused neurodegenerative disorders and the everyday ramifications of coming to terms with impending disability and new knowledge. They also consider some of the dynamics associated with the sometimes-stigmatizing effects of genetic disease.

3 Controlling destiny

"What's next?" is one of the core existential questions individuals face when confronted by major sickness or other types of life-changing misfortune. In her classic book, *Disrupted Lives: How People Create Meaning in a Chaotic World*, the late Gay Becker offers a road map to the ways that individuals come to accept and move beyond significant disruptions like the loss of a loved one, a major illness, infertility, financial upheaval, or some other break in the continuity of one's imagined or expected life-course (Becker 1997).

Based on many years of research with different groups in diverse parts of the U.S., Becker shows that people move through their lives with a certain set of explicit or implicit expectations for each phase; and that such expectations determine the meanings assigned to specific events and the roles they enact in the course of their everyday experiences. Inner chaos results from unmet expectations, as individuals try to alleviate the feelings of powerlessness, hopelessness, and depression that result. For Becker, these feelings come in response to the loss of their imagined future. Becker's message, however, is one of optimism, not despair. She found that study participants who were successful in creating a new sense of order had found ways to redefine the meaning of the disruptions they were experiencing to allow them to reconfigure their expectations of both themselves and the world: "Efforts to reorder the world after a disruption begin with the body and after a period of chaos . . . efforts to integrate past and present are initiated . . . [and] notions of order in daily life begin to resurface and take shape" (Becker 1997:136). Reestablishing a sense of continuity requires abandoning the newly impossible old life story, and constructing a new one consistent with the new circumstances. Until the future has been reorganized and given new meaning with an altered set of hopes and dreams, moving ahead is almost impossible (Capps and Ochs 1995; Ezzy 2000).

In the following case, we use Becker's framework to show how one man diagnosed with Friedreich's ataxia managed to redefine his expectations for the future and create new meaning. We describe the chaos his diagnosis created as he was forced to abandon not only his expectations, but also his most valued identity: the sense of manhood he derived from his professional achievements. We then detail how he went about creating a new set of expectations more consistent with his newly imagined future, although perhaps not wholly consonant with the actual reality that awaited him. In doing so, we show that while the patient sought to hide as many of the details about his diagnosis and prognosis as he could from those around him, it was not primarily because of the stigma of his genetic diagnosis but rather because he wanted a chance to design a new lifestyle before the disease could begin to alter the one he was living.

Friedreich's ataxia is an inherited motor neuron disease that causes progressive damage to the nervous system with wide ranging symptoms that include muscle weakness, speech problems, and heart disease. Like all ataxias, whether inherited or not, Friedreich's ataxia is associated with shaky and unsteady movements in the arms and legs. About 1 in 50,000 people in the U.S. have the condition, with both males and females affected in equal proportions. Difficulty walking, or gait ataxia, is usually the first symptom to appear, with onset typically between the ages of 5 and 15. At present there is no cure, although medications can help alleviate many of the symptoms. Like movement disorders in general, the rate of progression of Friedreich's ataxia varies from individual to individual, but due to muscle wasting, an affected person is generally confined to a wheelchair within 10 to 20 years after the initial appearance of symptoms; in its later stages, individuals become completely incapacitated. Most individuals with Friedreich's ataxia die in early adulthood, although some with less severe symptoms can live into their sixties or even seventies.

We chose Enrique Silvestre as part of our in-depth longitudinal sample because he was reflective, articulate, and eager to be part of the research. During the period in which we came to know Enrique, he seemed deeply lonely, having attenuated or cut off completely his two most important relationships in the wake of his diagnosis. He particularly interested us because he was among the handful of patients (Ana Almendra in Chapter 2 was another) who actively sought genetic testing, which he believed would help him "more quickly get to the bottom of things." This contrasts with most others in our study who might have harbored suspicions or even beliefs that their medical problems could be genetic, but were not actively seeking genetic testing. Our contact with Enrique consisted of two face-to-face meetings, eight telephone conversations, and four emails. They began about two months after his positive genetic test and continued for about a year until we finally lost contact with him.

Enrique's narrative reveals that ongoing ties to relatives in his home country, in concert with relationships he subsequently established in the U.S. with a business partner ("a man from a good family") and his fiancée ("a college educated girl") had enabled Enrique to begin to realize his "American Dream" of relative wealth and upward social mobility. The shock of his ataxia diagnosis forced him to reevaluate this plan and, ultimately, to abandon it in order to create a radically different one. To achieve this, Enrique forced himself to distance himself from his business partner and his fiancée so he would be "free to start a new life." During our period of most intense contact, we observed Enrique caught between his wish to hold on to his economic and social achievements – and his need to let them go in order to preserve something far more important – his sense of control and self-image of manhood and power.

To extricate himself from this dilemma Enrique sought to project the image of a man in command of his current and future situations. This was in fact his characteristic adaptation to life's challenges and opportunities. Despite the many uncertainties about his future capabilities, his detailed plans to start a new life back home showed him to still be in charge and intent on maintaining his independence. While Enrique's narrative was not always consistent with the likely future outcome of his situation, his perspective enabled him to create a new sense of meaning based on his changed life circumstances. His story illustrates Becker's profound insight that successful efforts to reorder one's world after a major break require reintegrating the past and present into a newly imagined future.

Background   *enrique*

When we met Enrique, he was 29 and had been living in the U.S. for nearly 10 years. Tall, well dressed, and assertive, he was proud of the considerable successes he had achieved since emigrating from South America as a teenager who had just finished high school. He reported coming from "a good family" (i.e. with resources and prestige) but that a series of financial missteps by a relative of his mother had nearly destroyed the family economically. He credited his father's business acuity with keeping them all from utter destitution. While Enrique seemed to idolize and strongly identify with his father, he was more ambivalent about his mother, who he described as "a poor soul, a sensitive woman who found refuge in music." She was "adored by everybody," Enrique explained, but could not imagine "what life would have been like for my sister and me had we not had my father's care. We couldn't count on [our mother], she was always suffering from depression." He expressed similar ambivalence toward Clara, his only sister, who he characterized as "the weakest link in my chain of relatives" (*el eslabon más débil de mi cadena de parientes*) and "someone always in need." He described their current relationship as emotionally distant but added, "She knows I'm always her brother and above all we're family." In a seeming parallel with his views about his mother, he faulted Clara for her "lack of energy," explaining that, "She had potential, but hasn't accomplished much in life."

Partly to flee his unhappy family situation, Enrique came to the U.S. to seek his fortune. With the backing of Emile Kelton, a business partner he met here, Enrique built "a small but successful" construction company. He told us that he also owned his own home and conspiratorially added that although his "declared" annual income was "only about $100,000, it's enough for a decent standard of living." He said that his business grew steadily thanks to his own vision and dedication, and that he had planned to expand prior to the decline of his health.

Nine months before we met Enrique, he had become engaged to marry, but broke off the engagement upon learning his diagnosis. He said he had done so not because he was concerned about passing the disease onto potential offspring, but because he believed he would soon be unable to fulfill the role of family breadwinner. In his view, a man should "maintain his wife like a princess" (i.e. shouldering 100 percent of the economic burden), thus when he was diagnosed with a neurodegenerative disease, marriage instantly became out of the question.

Aside from his fiancée, Enrique's closest relationship in the U.S. was with Emile, whom he regarded "as a brother, a man who may lack *agallas* [what it takes to make it], but with a golden heart." He told us that although it had been very painful to abandon his business and marriage plans (and the two people closest to him), he did not plan to dwell on the subject because "moaning and groaning is for losers."

Enrique's medical problems began around age 25. He vividly remembered the first sign of his illness: he was holding a toolbox and felt his arm grow numb, shortness of breath, and a general sense of weakness. He said that then and there, he was forced to stop what he was doing. As he did, he had a peculiar sensation: he "saw" in a kind of flash the face of a maternal uncle, and intuited that he was experiencing "something similar to him." But the internist who first evaluated Enrique thought otherwise, linking the episode to too much smoking and drinking, or as Enrique put it, "too much of the good life" (*una vida de vino, mujeres y canto*) and he advised Enrique to stop overindulging. The neurologist Enrique consulted around the same time also advised him to cut meat from his diet. He followed the first doctor's recommendations but drew the line at vegetarianism.

Enrique experienced no other significant health problems for three or four years until he fell from a ladder and began to experience problems walking. He sought advice from his primary care physician, to whom he explained that besides gait problems, he had begun to experience muscle pain and some sexual dysfunction. This doctor referred him to Dr Larea, a neurologist, who clinically diagnosed him with Friedreich's ataxia. A second neurologist agreed and added that the diagnosis could be confirmed by genetic testing. Enrique did not hesitate despite the $1,000 out-of-pocket cost. Sadly, the genetic test confirmed the worst.

From conversations with Dr Larea, Enrique understood the significance of his diagnosis and knew that his future had become uncertain. Still, for as long as we knew him, he painted a hopeful and optimistic picture. He told us that although he had been raised Catholic, he never "bought" the fatalistic precept that had guided his mother's existence that "life was a valley of tears." Instead, he emulated his father's belief that survival "favored the most fit." In the narratives that follow, we show that Enrique saw himself as one of them. He attributed his life's successes to a combination of good luck, a strong work ethic, and an unhesitating willingness to face life head on. He insisted that he intended to continue doing the same, even in the face of his diagnosis and the enormous uncertainty it created about what the future held in store.

Enrique's narrative

In the following text, extracted from our face-to-face meetings and phone conversations, "H.M.P" refers to the interviewer (H.M. Preloran) and "E.S." to Enrique.

5 April

H.M.P: You said you asked for the [genetic] test, [and then] you waited and waited and finally you got the results. And, then what happened?

E.S.:   I don't know where to start . . . You must know that I came here for the American dream. When I learned I had that [ataxia] my dream came crashing down . . . My [business] partner had come looking for me, I was at one of our construction sites and he told me that my doctor wanted to see me. I stopped [working] immediately and called him and then went to his office the same day . . . He told me that the test had come back positive and what they thought from the beginning [that it was Friedreich's ataxia] was confirmed. My first reaction? I told myself: "I have to grab the bull by the horns before it gets me!" (¡*Tengo que agarrar al toro por las astas antes que me pegue!*) [laughter]

H.M.P: What do you mean?

E.S.: That I have to take control before things get worse . . .

1 May

H.M.P: Were you able to take control?

E.S.: Yes, I made a "to do" list and I've already completed more than 80 percent of it! I'm the type of guy who can't sleep when there are things that need to be done . . . I did everything as I planned. Now I feel that everything is under control.

H.M.P: How [did you do it]? Did you get any help?

E.S.: No, I didn't need to. I did it all by myself – because I knew what I wanted and how I wanted to do it.

30 May

H.M.P: How have things been going?

E.S.: I feel okay. As soon as I felt that everything was under control here [in the States] and there [his native country] I could sleep better. And, so . . . not bad, I did practically all of it [i.e. selling his share of his business, his car, his home, and most of his other belongings; convincing an uncle to sell him half his farm and starting the paperwork to do so; arranging for his trip back home, and persuading his niece to begin building an addition onto her home] in a month.

H.M.P: How could you do all that [so quickly]?

E.S.: Good planning and better execution! [laughter] If you need someone to fix your problems call me [more laughter] . . . I'm very good at planning and it's easy if you have a clear vision of future, if you know where are you going . . .

H.M.P: Talking about the future . . . you told me that you were somewhat disappointed because you had expected a more concrete prognosis [in order to make plans] and you didn't get it.

E.S.: Right . . . that was kind of disappointing, but I saw [the future] more or less clearly anyway.

H.M.P: Did you read about [the prognosis]?

E.S.: No . . . but I had an idea of what to expect.

H.M.P: How, though?

E.S.: [silence]

5 June

H.M.P: At your last doctor's visit, did the neurologist explain anything new, because you said that now things are more or less clear for you?

E.S.:   No . . . I don't know how to explain it . . . But I think you'll understand. [After getting the diagnosis] I was . . . in my, I don't know how to say it . . . in my inner zone [laughter] thinking about how I could [reorganize my life], how could I restart it . . .

H.M.P: [Being in an] inner zone?

E.S.:   I have to explain [laughing] that I have a "gift" (*don*) . . . No, it's not a "gift." I don't want to call it . . . intuition . . . it's not intuition either . . .

H.M.P: Give me an example.

E.S.:   I don't talk about this because people may think I'm crazy, but, to be honest, that's what's helped me the most . . . Do you want me to tell you the whole story?

H.M.P: Of course!

E.S.:   Well, I believe that I'm a winner. I usually get good cards and I know how to play them. This is something natural, something that's part of me. And I believe it's because I have my good luck to thank . . . But I get things done mostly because I have a good head and I'm not afraid to work 24/7 . . . When I came [to the States] I was at an age when young men think only about girls. But I was determined to take advantage of the opportunities this country gives to immigrants and I focused on working.

H.M.P: You mentioned "intuition"? Does *it* help you play your cards?

E.S.:   Sometimes . . . yes. I can see things from my past, like flashing pictures, and I also see things that I think . . . could be from the future . . . I don't know if I should say predictions. . . . No, they're not predictions. They are things that are new to me, images I have never seen before and seeing them makes me think.

H.M.P: Are you a seer?

E.S.:   No! I told you it's difficult to explain. I don't want you to misunderstand me.

H.M.P: I think I understand. . . . You said you see images like flashing pictures and that they help you understand things and make you think.

E.S.:   Yes . . . more or less that's what happens . . . I may see an image a fraction of a second before something happens.

H.M.P: Now I'm somewhat lost. Do you mean that you could see, for example, an accident before it happens?

E.S.:   No, nothing like *that* ever happened to me. But for example, before I went to a DMV office for the first time, I "saw" in my mind an old typewriter. Crazy? Well, yes, but that's what I saw . . . And even more strange is that they only had computers everywhere in that office. But when I went up to the receptionist's desk there actually was an old typewriter on the floor, the same one I had seen in my mind.

H.M.P: Amazing . . . and how do you explain that?

E.S.:   I don't have an explanation. Even worse, most of the time [the images] don't mean anything. . . . They are coming and going for no reason . . . but other times the intuition helps. As I said, it doesn't happen all the time, but occasionally at work, I'm dealing with a client and I see something and I know, I have the intuition that something is not right. I feel that I have to take another road if I want to close the deal.

H.M.P.: Would you give me an example?

E.S.: One day my partner and I were a minute away from signing a big contract and I saw it. I saw my client opening the door of a very expensive car . . . I saw it in a flash . . . and I thought, "Something is wrong with this picture!" It may be that I knew that he wasn't a millionaire . . . I don't know, but I felt we needed to re-consider the contract. My partner was shocked, but he didn't object because he is easy and he would normally let me make the decisions. But from his expression I could tell that he was afraid. To make a long story short, less than a year later, this client filed for bankruptcy. And he destroyed one of our colleague's businesses in the process. I don't want to call this . . . intuition exactly. But the funny thing is that I don't go around telling people that I see things . . . but people say I have a good head for business . . . Many times my partner has told me that I was the brains of our company. Certainly he contributed the seed money to start but I made it grow. And when I told him I wanted to transfer my part of the business to him and that he could pay me at his convenience, he was grateful. He said, "This [offer] saved me because if I had to pay you all at once I couldn't do it."

H.M.P.: You must feel proud that the business went so well and you could allow your partner to pay at his convenience.

E.S.: I may sound arrogant, but yes . . . I feel great. I feel I created the company, the ideas were mine; my energy is what made the company what it is today . . . and now I can pass the torch.

H.M.P.: Right . . . [When you leave] will you stay in contact [with your business partner]?

E.S.: In contact, yes . . . but I won't be involved . . . It will be his company. But I believe that passing the torch in this way will keep things as they are . . . The other day I said to my partner, "I won't be here physically, but don't worry, I'll leave everything in order and will write down step-by-step how things should be done . . ." And I told him to tell the boys [employees] that I decided to go abroad to improve my economic situation.

H.M.P.: Do they know you're ill?

E.S.: Yes. They knew I was seeing doctors but I didn't tell them the prognosis; there is no reason to seek their pity. I want to leave them with the image of the Enrique they knew (*con el recuerdo del Enrique que conocieron*) . . .

6 June

H.M.P.: I called you many times this week and I couldn't reach you. I know that many things have happened during these past few days and that you're very busy. I want to know if everything is going well.

E.S.: Everything is under control! [laughter]

H.M.P: That sounds very "American"! [laughter]

E.S.:   [laughing] That's my "gringo" side. But seriously, that's my motto. When I came to this country, I said to myself, "I'm going to enter through the big door" and as the Constitution here says, I'm coming here in the pursuit of happiness.

H.M.P: Did you achieve happiness?

E.S.:   Aha . . . I think I achieved a lot, I can't complain.

H.M.P: It's nice to talk with you because you are always very optimistic and focused on your gains rather than your losses.

E.S.:   As my father would say, "Be thankful for your gains and learn from your losses."

7 June

H.M.P: Enrique, you mentioned your father several times in our conversations and always with great admiration. How old were you when he died?

E.S.:   It was shortly before I decided to come to the States.

H.M.P: You were still in your teens?

E.S.:   Yes.

H.M.P: And he seems to have been an influential figure in your life.

E.S.:   Absolutely . . . He was a strong man and I looked up to him. He was always talking about his projects, he was involved in politics; I don't remember him complaining . . . I try to do the same . . . When I had the accident, that fall from the ladder, after that I began to have one problem after another . . . I told you about the muscle pain, the walking problems, sexual dysfunction, but I told my girlfriend "Everything will be okay" . . . [But] I knew [then and there] that the old Enrique had died. I knew we were going to break up, but what else was I going to do? But I [also] knew I would be like the phoenix that is reborn from its ashes [laughter]. (*Sabía que el viejo Enrique había muerto. Sabía que terminaríamos rompiendo, ¿pero qué iba a hacer? También sabía que soy como el Ave Fenix que renace de las cenizas.*)

H.M.P: You are always looking on the bright side!

E.S.:   Well, what good will come from crying over what's lost? I always said to my boys [employees] "A bird in the hand is worth two in the bush!" (*¡Mejor pájaro en mano que cien volando!*)

H.M.P: That's pure pragmatism. Could it be that your positive attitude came from your intuition or your "visions"? [And] tell me, would it be okay to call those images you mentioned . . . "visions"?

E.S.:   It's perfect! I never thought to call them visions, once I thought that I had a photographic memory that covered the past and the future [laughter], but visions sounds good!

H.M.P: And you said those visions come when you are in your inner zone.

E.S.:   Yes . . . well, sometimes . . . I'd say yes . . . some ideas come when I am thinking . . . alone, concentrating inside myself . . .

H.M.P.: Would you give me an example? You told me that when you came from the doctor's office you were already making some decisions. Those came from your inner zone?

E.S.: When I knew the truth [the day he was informed of the positive genetic test], I have to tell you . . . It was big . . . I saw many things. . . .

H.M.P.: Really? That was when the doctor told you that you had the ataxia?

E.S.: [Later] . . . when I left the hospital, I looked for the best cigars money can buy and I bought them. And that afternoon, although I don't usually drink at lunch hour, I opened a bottle of brandy reserved for special occasions. The thing I remember most vividly was the change in light. The room went from bright to dark. I sat in front of a window; my mind was blank. But I noticed the day was passing by . . . because of the light. Little by little the room grew dark and I saw pictures, flashing pictures . . . That's what I remember. They were kind of visions like you said. I was in those pictures: my birthday, my trip to Hawaii . . . I was having a good time. And then, I saw a picture, a picture of a wheelchair.

H.M.P.: Only a wheelchair?

E.S.: I saw myself in the wheelchair . . .

H.M.P.: That would be shocking

E.S.: [silence]

H.M.P.: And that was all [you saw]?

E.S.: No, then, I saw a farm . . . my uncle's farm. I used to spend summers there. I saw old images and new ones: good food, good wine, nights of candle-light and guitar playing and singing . . . And I said to myself, "Enrique, if that's where you are going . . . it's not too bad!"

H.M.P.: [The other day] you told me that you bought half that farm. That was before or after you got your [genetic] diagnosis . . . after the visions?

E.S.: After . . . I made most of the changes that I told you about . . . after, after I knew the truth. . . . The doctor said that there is no guarantee . . . I may have five years, ten years . . . twenty, who knows [before becoming completely incapacitated]. So I said to myself, "Life on the farm looks okay." I knew then that I needed to liquefy all my assets, get as much cash as possible and move on to a new life . . . I knew that with my money I would be a Rockefeller [in my home country] and you know . . . I'll be okay. Money is power. I could create a good life for myself. I could do whatever I pleased. I'd take advantage of the years I felt okay and then take it from there . . . I thought it would be a good move and I said to myself, "Go for it!" [Besides] I have many things in common with my uncle: we're bachelors and free as birds, and we, as the lyric goes, we both love wine, women, and song!

H.M.P.: Yes . . . wine, women, and song, but you didn't mention women in your visions.

E.S.: Right! [There are no] women . . . but who knows for how long! [laughter] There may not be anyone now, but over there I might find someone who wants to be with me. Here it's different. Here, without working, I'd be a nobody. But over there, I can live comfortably. We have to hold on to our hope.

H.M.P: After the [genetic] diagnosis you made a lot of changes . . . And although you always talk about them positively, I imagine that some must have been painful.

E.S.: Of course.

H.M.P: I wonder whether finding out the truth [i.e. agreeing to the test] was worthwhile?

E.S.: Absolutely. You've asked me that question several times and I keep repeating, "Yes" [it was worthwhile]. And let me add this: having that test [available] and not offering it to patients would be a sin . . . It offers the possibility to build the last years of your life as you wish . . . It gives you control over your life; it gives you freedom.

Discussion

Enrique Silvestre's narrative illustrates Becker's core insight that recovery after a major life disruption can depend on constructing a new life story. Her argument is that time takes on a different meaning before and after the crisis, as hopes, dreams, prospects, and plans are reevaluated in light of a foreshortened or otherwise transformed future (Becker 1997: 37). She also notes that the particular form healing narratives take are to a large degree shaped by culture. In the case of her study participants in the U.S., she found that the ability to successfully come to terms with traumatic disruptions involved the construction of stories that placed a great emphasis on continuity.

Others have shown that healing narratives must be rooted in an individual's biography, psychology, and earlier life experiences in order to be meaningful and effective (Bury 1982; Garro 1992; Mathews, Lannin, and Mitchell 1994). Enrique's accounts demonstrate this precisely. We saw that throughout his medical ordeal and concerns about an uncertain future, he sought to maintain his self-image as a man with enormous self-control and the master of his destiny. This self-image seems in part to reflect his father's rationality and Social Darwinian worldview – and appears to be a complete rejection of what he perceived as his mother's extreme sensitivity that had disastrous consequences for the family. Other key threads of continuity in Enrique's narration include his identification with his father, both like phoenixes, reborn from their own ashes: his father had rescued and restored the family economically after devastating economic losses, and Enrique, through good luck and hard work, had achieved the "American Dream."

Constructing a potent narrative (for oneself and for others) can offer unexpected difficulties when the narrator is pulled by impulses that reflect contradictory experiences, views of, and approaches to life. During our many conversations with Enrique, despite our best efforts to explore his thoughts and feelings about his health, medical experiences, and larger life situation, he often responded in terms of recent or past successful business transactions. He was preoccupied with projecting an image that showcased his economic achievements, the struggles he'd endured to "make it" in the U.S., and the strategies he had developed to maintain his standard of living once he returned to his home country. Enrique's ataxia diagnosis clearly posed an enormous threat to his sense of control. He told us repeatedly that he had sought genetic testing in order to get "to the bottom of things" and learn "the truth" (that is, an accurate diagnosis) as soon as possible, so he could "take the bull by the horns." He explained that he had "inherited" his father's take-charge approach to life with the illustration that when his mother became ill, his father promptly sought a number of medical opinions because "even if there is bad news, knowing always helps" (*aunque la noticia sea mal, el conocimiento siempre ayuda*). In other words, for Enrique, knowledge unquestionably is power.

Further evidence of the importance of rationality and self-control was seen in Enrique's reluctance to discuss the emotional losses consequent to his diagnosis. When we touched on those issues, he made them appear less important by explaining that the break-up with his girlfriend was sad, but to be expected (*se veía venir*), since in its final months their relationship had been "going sour." He optimistically added that he hadn't given up on the idea that he would someday find another romantic partner because "there is someone for everyone" (*nunca falta un roto para un descocido*). On a different occasion, he speculated that his wealth would help him find new romance. With regard to Emile, his business partner who was "like a brother," he minimized the significance of dissolving their business relationship by saying that they would stay in touch and that he would be leaving a set of suggestions for keeping the company healthy.

Still, despite considerable consistency in Enrique's stories, close analysis revealed significant contradictions. On one hand, his responses to direct questions depicted a powerful man with enormous self-control (e.g. seeking out genetic testing for a quick and hopefully definitive diagnosis, making major irrevocable personal and economic decisions). But there was also another side, suggesting understandable fear, insecurity, and weakness. This was evidenced by Enrique's decision to hide from his family, employees, and friends the fact that he was afflicted with a neurodegenerative disease that in time would become incapacitating. He explained this by saying he wanted to avoid pity and, more specifically, did not want to frighten his sister Clara, because if she knew the seriousness of his condition, she might make the "bad decision" to move to the States to take care of him. He had not yet focused on the potential ramifications of his genetic diagnosis for his beloved niece.

We found Enrique's explanation that he was withholding information about his diagnosis to keep others from worrying or feeling sorry for him not entirely convincing. We believe he was masking the truth (even from himself) because above all, he needed to maintain his self-image of power, control, and mastery for as long as possible. He knew and likely feared that he would begin to lose at least some of his independence in the not-too-distant future, and thus was making detailed plans to transfer authority over his health, finances, and his overall future to his sister. But he had not yet told her he was doing so.

This neat duality obscures a more complicated reality. After an accidental fall worsened his emerging symptoms, Enrique acted as his father might have: he immediately searched for an accurate diagnosis, requested a genetic test, and rationally, it seemed, began planning for his eventual disability. But his actual decision-making process appeared to also be guided by his mother's more emotional and intuitive approach: all of his important new decisions (i.e. the right time to move, the best place to move to, with whom he should plan to live) were based on "pictures" or "visions" seen or experienced in his "inner zone."

Our efforts to probe into the meaning of the "vision" Enrique saw of an uncle when he was experiencing what eventually proved to be his own first ataxia symptoms were not very productive. In his answer to our standard interview question, "Are any of your relatives also affected with movement disorder symptoms?," Enrique mentioned only the same uncle, one of his mother's brothers, but was not sure about the cause of his uncle's problem: only that his gait was "strange" and he ended up in a wheelchair before he died.

From various comments, we knew Enrique intended to foreground his self-image of rationality and control for as long as possible. When asked if he had had similar visions when he was younger and whether he had ever told his father of them, he changed the subject and did not answer. This led us to conclude he might well have had such images and not told his father – perhaps because he believed that his father would not approve of his use of "images" in making critical life decisions. Enrique was also unwilling to discuss how he came upon these "pictures" that formed the basis for his future plans. He said that besides us, he did not talk about "those things" because he could be misunderstood or considered "flaky." And whenever he did bring them up, he employed a confidential tone and sometimes laughed self-consciously, as if he himself was not taking what he was telling us all that seriously. Nevertheless, it was his visions that lay at the center of his story, and which were the subject he spent the most time discussing as our relationship deepened.

Also significantly, during our many conversations, Enrique barely mentioned his sister Clara or her adult daughter, Dora. In the immediate period prior to his departure, Enrique indicated that he would be moving directly to the farm. He explained that he had decided on this course because in contrast with his many relatives on his mother's side, he and this uncle had a lot in common. But for the first time, he added that he also intended to use Clara's home in the capital as a pied-à-terre.

Scattered bits of information when eventually tied together indicated that immediately after his diagnosis, Enrique decided he would, indeed, involve Clara in his care. He put her name on the title to the farm he was buying and offered Dora, who lived with her mother, money to build an addition onto their family's home. He described his phone conversation with Dora, in which he told us he "tempted" her with an offer: the new space would give her yearned-for privacy and more control over her own life, and would also be available for Enrique to use on his occasional visits to town. Interestingly, he told no one else of this plan. Instead, his public story was that he expected to live on the farm indefinitely and move to the city much later, representing himself in the role in which he was most comfortable: that of "giver" rather than "taker."

All this led us to believe that Enrique was torn by contradictory emotions and feelings of uncertainty to a much greater extent than he admitted. Creating a post-diagnosis narrative that portrayed him as a "winner" may have helped Enrique sustain the identity he most valued after it had been severely dashed by his diagnosis of Friedreich's ataxia. However, he had, in fact, also placed his destiny and that of his beloved company in the hands of "weak" individuals – his sister and his business partner.

An email from Enrique several months after he had returned to his home country disclosed that his plans had not unfolded quite as the public story he had created beforehand. Instead of going directly to the countryside, he spent his first six months living in Clara's home. He rationalized this extended visit by saying he wanted to take advantage of the resources a big city offered: "I stayed longer [than I'd intended] so I could leave all the papers in order," he wrote. These included granting Clara a general power of attorney.

Enrique's story reveals the processes through which he received a definitive diagnosis for his movement disorder symptoms, came to terms with the gravity of his situation, created a radically revised set of future expectations, and a new life narrative to facilitate them. Like Ana Almendra in Chapter 2, genetic testing quickly and efficiently gave Enrique critical information and dramatically reduced the uncertainty with which he was living.

Enrique had sought genetic testing not because he was interested in learning whether his symptoms were hereditary (he apparently had no real context for thinking that they might be), but because he believed it would provide the most definitive diagnosis possible (*yo pedí un estudio lo más completo possible*) and that the information would enable him to best plan for and accommodate to his future limitations. And similarly, subsequently learning that an inherited gene was the cause of his disease was not in any way transformational for him. Like many patients in this study, the main thing that a genetic diagnosis signified for Enrique was that his disease was incurable. But in Enrique's case, we found this particularly intriguing because of the strength of his identification with his parents. More so than many study participants, Enrique's sense of self-identity and beliefs about who and what he had become were deeply informed by his strong positive identification with his father's character and rejection of all that was his mother's.

Enrique's story highlights the sometimes-contradictory processes brought into play when one or a series of life-altering experiences threatens or frankly challenges an individual's sense of self. Enrique repeatedly attributed his life achievements to his masculine drive, determination, and rational approach to problem solving, and approached his impending disability in the very same way. In doing so, he relegated to the background the more feminine intuition that had, in fact, figured prominently in his decisions. This strategy enabled Enrique to preserve the image and narrative of independence, even as he knew that before too long, he would need to be cared for and protected. He resolved this contradiction through an elaborate plan that potentially offered years of independence – but with the security of a sheltered refuge awaiting him. During our final phone conversations and in emails during the months after returning home, Enrique again sounded happy with his achievements and plans.

We offer this chapter as a contribution to research on narratives as therapeutic tools for patients with progressive neurodegenerative disorders, and other serious illnesses, in which core identity is profoundly threatened. What is unique lies in our effort to consider the consequences of the fact that a defective gene was the cause of Enrique's worsening symptoms. We saw that while the actual diagnosis was less important to Enrique than its consequences, his diagnosis did precipitate an intense process of self-reflection and reformulation of his life's plans, including his decision to abandon his plan to marry and father children.

In Chapter 4, we'll see that Carlos Estrada's genetic diagnosis was vastly more meaningful than Enrique's. Like Enrique, Carlos's diagnosis forced him to alter his life plans and reimagine his future but unlike Enrique, who uncritically accepted the immutability of his diagnosis, Carlos's transformed its meaning over time. Also, in comparison with Enrique who showed little concern about the stigmatizing potential of a genetic diagnosis, for Carlos, who had suffered movement disorder symptoms since childhood and whose siblings were also affected, stigma was a much more central feature of his illness experience.

influential

4 Dream of a new life

In this chapter we offer narratives told by some of the members of a Mexican immigrant family in which two sisters and a brother all experience symptoms of a progressive neurodegenerative disorder. We analyze the effects of the symptoms on their daily lives and their abilities to fulfill their roles, goals, and dreams in spite of their physical limitations. While we consider the experiences of a mother and her three children, we focus mainly on Carlos, the family's only son. As the sole male member and eldest child, he suffered a crisis of confidence as his symptoms intensified because he was no longer able to function as chief breadwinner. As a result of his inability to meet his own role expectations, he grew increasingly withdrawn from both his family and the larger society. Still, over time, he came to terms with his debilitating symptoms and began to create a new vision for his own and his family's future.

Since it is axiomatic that genetics concerns kinship and families, it is surprising that aside from a handful of notable exceptions (e.g. Cox and McKellin 1999; Featherstone, Atkinson, Bharadwaj, and Clarke 2005; Finkler 2000; Sorenson and Botkin 2003) there has been little research on the consequences of the new genetics for families and family relationships. After an exhaustive review of the literature on the subject, Peterson concludes that, "the role of family issues in determining health behaviors and outcomes related to genetic counseling and testing has not been well studied, and in fact, may differ from other areas [of medicine]" (Peterson 2005: 628). Instead, most work by social scientists has focused on the individuals directly afflicted. This, in part, is due to the difficulties involved in conceptualizing the family for research purposes, given the nature and extent of its variable forms (Peterson 2005; Van Riper 2005). Researchers are also perhaps deterred by the methodological complexities of obtaining detailed data from or about more than one member of a given group. Our culture's changing values may also be contributing factors as we increasingly regard the individual, not the group, as the most important and valuable social unit.

Still, few of us live in a social vacuum, and medical problems in general, and chronic ones in particular, tend to have significant consequences not simply for a sick person but for everyone else in the immediate social environment. To better comprehend these consequences, we broadly draw upon Kazak and colleagues' family systems contextual approach for studying the impact of chronic illness on family life (Kazak, Segal-Andrews, and Johnson 1995; see also Patterson and Garwick 1994; Ross, Mirowsky, and Goldsteen 1990). But whereas their framework concerns children and families with only one sick member, here we expand it to adults and the experiences and adaptations of three ill siblings.

We will show that the ramifications of the effects of chronic illness are likely more profound if the illness is discovered to be genetic. Beyond a merely chronic disorder, hereditary disease can evoke unique issues of responsibility and obligation. Blood relatives, in particular, feel a special sense of obligation because it is within the family that we form our core identity and learn to interact with others (Callanan and LeRoy 2006; Richards 1996). To a far greater extent than non-genetic illness, a genetic diagnosis can seriously strain or even rupture family relationships, as well as transform the way we regard our ancestors and descendents.

Although a genetic diagnosis is often considered in a special category because of its stigmatizing potential (Green and Botkin 2003; Sankar *et al.* 2006) and implications for other family members (Bird and Bennett 1995; Burke, Pinsky, and Press 2001; Hallowell 1999), we will show that under certain circumstances, a genetic diagnosis can be legitimatizing by providing a long-elusive explanation for the inability to fulfill normal social roles and expectations. Yet, as we shall see, in and of itself, the genetic diagnosis did little to generate optimism for family members whose lives were becoming increasingly disrupted by deteriorating health. Instead, for one of the siblings, the diagnosis simply did not make sense and it was ignored. For the second, although it was welcomed because it could be used to justify cutting back on family responsibilities and obligations, it simultaneously intensified fears about its implications for the health of future generations. And for the third sibling, more meaningful than being told by doctors that they attributed his and his sisters' symptoms to a genetic disorder was the opportunity their diagnoses offered for him to reimagine his future and begin to chart a path for an uncertain life ahead.

Background

Carlos Estrada, a 47-year-old man of Mexican origin, migrated with his mother and two sisters to southern California more than 30 years earlier. The family was poor, rural, worked in agriculture, and was abandoned by the father while the children were still young. Our data come from six face-to-face conversations with Carlos and two conversations each with Eduarda, his mother, and Maria, the older of his two sisters, plus three telephone conversations with Carlos, and three each with Eduarda and Maria over a period of about a year. We repeatedly tried to communicate with Silvia, the younger sister, but she had recently married, moved away, and had somewhat distanced herself from the rest of the family, particularly Carlos, which made contacting her practically impossible.

The three siblings manifested symptoms of a progressive muscle disorder that began affecting them during childhood, but each to a different degree. Silvia, 35, had the most serious problems, while Maria, age 40, was least affected. Carlos, the eldest, had seen his symptoms increase in severity in recent years. His worsening tremors cost him his most recent job in a restaurant – and led him to our study.

The 20-minute medical evaluation where we met Carlos revolved mainly around a discussion of his symptoms, diagnosis, and treatment options. Still, most of the comments he himself initiated during that consultation (as well as in subsequent conversations) focused on his concerns about being unemployed and without health insurance. The neurologist tried to ease Carlos's worries by saying that a genetic diagnosis could greatly help him make a successful case for disability benefits.

The consultation

Carlos arrived at Dr Larea's general neurology clinic having been clinically diagnosed by doctors in Mexico and the U.S. as suffering from Spinal Muscular Atrophy (SMA). He had been referred to Dr Larea by the internist he had recently begun seeing. SMA is an autosomal recessive genetic disease (which means that both parents of an affected individual must be carriers of the abnormal gene and both must have passed the gene on to their child). SMA is characterized by progressive muscle weakness resulting in degeneration and loss of horn cells in the spinal cord and stem nuclei. Those affected either never acquire or progressively lose the ability to walk, stand, and sit, and eventually lose the ability to move entirely. Cognition, intellect, emotional development, and sensory nerves remain unaffected. While SMA patients can benefit from symptomatic treatments, there are no known drugs to alter its progression.

There are several classifications of the disease mainly established by the age of onset, ranging from prenatal (SMA 0) to adult onset (SMA V). Dr Larea diagnosed Carlos as SMA V because "he experienced the first clear symptoms when he was in his twenties" and because Carlos was also experiencing severe sleep problems and joint pain, complications usually associated with SMA V. Because other relatives had similar symptoms, and because Carlos wanted to pursue his disability claim, Dr Larea suggested that Carlos "could start to think about having a genetic test." Carlos readily agreed.

Dr Larea himself did not offer genetic testing and referred Carlos to a more specialized facility. He was pleased that his assistant was able to book Carlos an appointment for testing within a month, and was relieved to learn that the genetics clinic would accept Carlos's limited medical insurance and also provide genetic counseling. Later, the doctor explained that he did not feel very comfortable discussing genetic testing. Knowing that patients would have the option of counseling when he referred them elsewhere made him feel "more at ease" in making genetics referrals.

As we shall see, Carlos's perceptions of the course of his illness and his experiences with SMA were very different from Dr Larea's assessments of Carlos's situation. In this regard, like Ana's, his experience can be seen to illustrate the often-profound gap between illness and disease. For Carlos, the onset of symptoms did not begin in his twenties: he had been having problems walking "as long as [he could] remember." And, as we discuss later, this difference in perception as to the initial onset of the illness may not only have affected the diagnosis process, but the development of treatment strategies as well. Like Mattingly (1998), we will argue that the time frame in which a storyteller, in our case the patient, places the succession of events helps to shape the meaning of the situation. For Dr Larea, Carlos was a clear case of an SMA V diagnosis with a happy ending, since the positive genetic test would enable him to receive permanent disability benefits. For Carlos, the prospect of finally having a definitive diagnosis and prognosis for problems that had plagued him since childhood only reinforced the growing feelings of dependency he had long sought to avoid.

Family context

Throughout our conversations with Carlos, his mother, and his sister, we tried to keep the focus on Carlos and his family's experiences in seeking a diagnosis and treatment. But they all, and especially Carlos, frequently framed those experiences within the context of their consequences for Carlos's role as head of the family. For him and the other relatives we talked to, the center of the narrative was Carlos's inexorable journey toward physical and economic dependence. The family's individual accounts about their efforts to help maintain Carlos's independence and self-esteem led us to believe that those were the topics most meaningful to them.

Although Carlos's symptoms were not the most severe of the three siblings, his disability defined his childhood to a much greater extent than it did for either of his sisters. This was a pattern that continued into adulthood. Despite their physical limitation, both sisters attended school, helped their mother at home, and eventually married. Maria had become the mother of two teenage sons. In contrast, as a child, Carlos felt marginalized, socially isolated, and insecure. He barely finished elementary school and never married. Instead, he devoted himself to supporting his mother and sisters until the younger women left home to take up lives of their own. Compensating perhaps for his social difficulties, Carlos relished his self-styled role as "head of the family," recounting with considerable pride and satisfaction having helped his adult sisters with sage brotherly advice, as well as economically during periods when their husbands were unemployed and their own resources insufficient. We argue that Carlos's view of himself as head of the family, formed at a very young age after his father abandoned them, became core to his adult identity and sense of wellbeing. Knowing this helps explain why his worsening symptoms and concomitant loss of job and income were so demoralizing, that even the prospect of his successful disability claim and the financial security it would provide offered little solace.

The narratives below are drawn from our conversations with Carlos, Maria, and their mother, Eduarda, and are offered chronologically. On several occasions when we sought to speed up the conversation or were not sure where Carlos was heading, as was our experience with Ana Almendra, Carlos insisted on chronologically sequenced narrations, which in his case were anchored by his own age at the time of the events in question.

Family narratives

Carlos: I'm 47 years old now but I have been suffering as long as I can remember. My mom says that since I was a baby I had difficulties walking. She thought I was retarded and lazy because I crawled until I was 2 or so. [Later] I knew that something was wrong with me because when I was a child, I couldn't play soccer. I didn't have friends. My schoolmates didn't want to be with me. [Eventually] my problem got worse and I found it hard to climb steps. That was when I was 30 . . . but before, when I was 17, almost 18 or later, I couldn't walk well . . . people thought I was drunk! But that is another story and the important thing is that in one way or another, I always managed to take care of my family (*para las tortillas siempre había*).

During that conversation, Carlos repeatedly mentioned his mother and his fears about the implications of his deteriorating health for their economic security, along with the concern she kept expressing about his tendency to isolate himself socially. We asked to meet her in order to get her perspective on the experiences of Carlos and the rest of their family with SMA. It initially proved difficult to arrange a face-to-face meeting, but after about a month and several phone conversations, we succeeded in scheduling an appointment. During that meeting, we learned that Eduarda's worries revolved primarily around her children, Carlos and Silvia, and the increasing disruption their worsening SMA symptoms were having on their relationships with one another.

Eduarda: Not one day passes without me crying. I asked God to free my children of such pain and put it on me. It breaks my heart to see Carlos walking . . . he has a lot of pride and he pretends to be okay . . . but he keeps stumbling and lately he has fallen several times . . . he doesn't let me help him get out of bed. Only [his sister] Maria is able to help him a little; they are very close. Actually we all are very close, but Silvia, since she moved, has become somewhat distant. And she has her own [medical] problems . . . When my husband left, Carlos became head of the family. He gave me every penny he made to take care of us.

She added that although her son was still managing to support their household, because of progressively increasing tremors in recent years, he had not been earning as much as in the past.

As our conversations with Carlos continued on a weekly basis, we gained a deeper understanding of the ways in which his illness had affected his sense of self worth. We also came to see that Carlos's narrative strategy involved using his childhood and adolescence to provide a framework for interpreting his current medical experiences (cf. Garro and Mattingly 2000).

Carlos: Back in Mexico, I was more or less okay. I worked in the fields [and] I could take care of my family. [I said] more or less because I always felt different. One of my defects is that I'm very timid and I haven't had luck with girls. [One day] I got a girl who loved me, but her mother saw me walking and she freaked out! She told her daughter, "How can you think of marrying him, don't you see he is defective?" So my girl left me and I didn't look for another woman because I knew that it would be the same. That hurt a lot . . . I knew I couldn't have my own family. Luckily, my sister gave me nephews. [But] now [with the positive genetic test result] I'm worried for them too. I don't want them to be incomplete [as men] . . . not to have children [like me] . . . no family of their own.

Reflecting on his past, he noted with pride:

I was always a good worker. When we came [to the U.S.] it took me six months to find a good job but I found one and I made good money. But, for the last 30 years, my health has been so-so . . . and it is getting worse and worse. Lately I began to have tremors in my hands constantly . . . and I can't hold onto the pots [in a restaurant kitchen where he worked] so I had to get disability . . . [Referring to his fulltime job in that restaurant] My mother was happy for me and I was happy because I could take care of her. [In those days] I could also help my sisters although [eventually] they got married . . . but my brothers-in-law got laid off a couple of times and I helped them . . . [It] all ended with my disability. I don't want to sound ungrateful, like my mother says . . . I appreciate the government's help. It's helping us with my medical bills and home expenses. But it's so little that it hardly lasts until the end of the month. I used to pay for Silvia's bus fare when she came to visit, but I can't anymore . . . that's gone. [And now] we don't see much of each other. We're somewhat distant; she doesn't pay attention to me [as she did before].

In our first face-to-face meeting with Eduarda, we were intrigued by her account of the deepening bond she saw forming between her older daughter, Maria, and Carlos, as Carlos's SMA symptoms worsened. This was a bittersweet situation for Eduarda, since she was feeling that her own relationship with Carlos was diminishing. Still, she expressed great satisfaction in the way Maria was managing her own SMA symptoms and the positive role model this provided for Carlos and her grandchildren. We asked whether we might talk with Maria. When we did, we learned that her immediate concerns were quite different from Carlos's.

Maria: What I'd like to know is whether [these symptoms we have] can be stopped because I realize that I'm getting worse and worse. I have less strength in my hands, less strength when I try to grasp something . . . I'm becoming more like my brother and sister, who were always sicker than I . . . I wish to see if it can be stopped, not keep advancing . . . And [I'd like to know] whether my children will also get sick. This is my great fear. This is a worry that's constantly on my mind because I can assure you that this is very, very hard, this disease we have. I want to know if my children are affected. They're not really children anymore, they're grown, and I want to know if they'll also have this problem.

Before they received the results of the genetic tests we asked one of our standard interview questions: "Do you have any fear of a genetic diagnosis, to be told once and for all that this is something in your family?"

Maria: No, frankly I'm so accustomed to this sickness, it's very shameful . . . If they would say to me that this sickness comes from the family in a certain form, it would be a relief. Because everyone would see once and for all that we're not lying (*engañando*). Everyone would know what I'm saying, that I'm not fooling anybody. And I'd be reassured, with one hundred percent security that I'll have a written certification that says that this is what I have! Fear, of course one is fearful and I'd like it not to be something in the family because of my kids . . . That would be a terrible blow knowing that this could happen to them too. And then my kids would also become worried . . . But honestly, we're already worried because we know this *has to be* in the family . . . a problem like this can't *not be*, what with three siblings with the same problem.

Three months later, we met with Eduarda again. We had learned from Maria that she had become even more concerned about Carlos's social isolation.

Eduarda: I'm happy that Carlos became friends with you. He is very timid and he doesn't open up easily, but he said he likes to discuss his doubts with you. I don't know if he told you that he is getting depressed lately, his mood has changed because he can't take care of us like he did before. I told him not to worry . . . but it doesn't work. He has become more and more isolated. When first I told him we could manage to live on his disability [benefit] he was very unhappy; he is very proud! He said it was like getting alms. Now he is okay with the disability benefits; he even asked his sister to apply. . . . But last year when I first asked him to consider [applying] he told me: "I'm not a beggar." He is grateful for the help we get from the government, but he was better when he could take care of the family with his work.

During the period of our contact with Eduarda, we also noticed her preoccupation with her son's increasing emotional volatility; on one occasion she even asked us if we could encourage him to be more patient and try to avoid confrontations with those around him.

Eduarda: More and more lately, my son has become very sensitive. Many things irritate him: when people give him a seat on the bus; when he needs to wait long hours to see a doctor. A few months ago [frustrated by the long wait] he was going to just get up and walk out of the office. But thank God, the receptionist stopped him and convinced him to wait a little longer. He complains, "Doctors are selfish, they only think about money, they don't want to spend time with you, they don't explain what's wrong with you. They ask for the tests and then don't say a word. Do they think I'm stupid? That because I'm sick, that I can't understand?" I tell him to be patient and not get angry, but he doesn't listen – when he's like this, he won't listen to anyone. Maybe he'd pay attention to you [ethnographers].

On more than one occasion, Eduarda told us that Carlos had always been proud of the fact that he had helped his family get ahead despite his illness, but that lately she's noticed that he doesn't act so proud anymore. She thought it could have something to do with his conviction that people had lost respect for him because he was getting state disability benefits and not working anymore.

Eduarda: Carlos thinks that those who can't work don't get respect from society. He believes that because he's not working, people look at him differently, like with indifference or pity. This is why he thinks now that everyone is against him, because he can't work, so he gets very touchy.

As we continued to spend time with the family, we came to better appreciate the deep sense of anxiety and confusion Carlos and Maria faced in light of testing positive for a genetic disease, which was understandable given their very limited knowledge about genetics and inherited disease. It was difficult for Eduarda and her children to comprehend that it was possible to inherit a disease whose symptoms manifested not at birth, but later in life, or that the carrier of a faulty gene could pass it on to his or her children – but not themselves show symptoms. We also learned that although the siblings had been treated by a significant number of different specialists over the years, and many, if not all, had suggested the possibility that they were suffering from an inherited disorder, none had ever referred them for genetic counseling.

Carlos: I have two sisters. I'm the oldest, the youngest is 35, and the one in the middle is 40. When you have two sisters and they suffered like you, well, you wonder [if it could be genetic]. The youngest is the one that [physically] suffers the most, but she didn't want the genetic test. She had seen doctors in Mexico and they told her that she also had SMA and that it was hereditary. But she didn't believe [that we got it from our parents] because we got sick when we were older and our parents were healthy, they were not like us . . . Besides, when we were young, we were more or less okay . . . We have been getting worse and worse since we are here [in the U.S.].

Maria: We thought that it was odd [referring to the Mexican doctor's explanation that their illness could be genetic] because my parents were always healthy. How could it be hereditary? But, now that we have the tests results for me and Carlos, now we can't deny it . . . right?

While Carlos did not fully comprehend the significance of their genetic diagnosis, he recognized that it would have profound consequences for his position both within his family group and in the larger society.

Carlos: Getting the genetic test results for me was . . . the beginning of the end because things changed. Silvia does not listen to me anymore. So, I left her alone . . . I don't call her . . . nothing . . . and I've become closer to my other sister. But most of the time I'm alone in my room. My mother insisted that I go out to see people. So I enrolled in an English class, but I'm not sure if I will be able to learn because my mind is not what it used to be.

Nevertheless, Carlos's greatest fears continued to revolve around losing power within his own family. What upset him most about being unable to hold a job and becoming more physically impaired was a disturbing paradox: as he felt himself becoming increasingly irrelevant to his family, he was also becoming more dependent on them.

Maria and I had the same [physical] problems . . . we can't walk; it's hard to sleep; Silvia, poor girl, got it worse. She can't breathe; it's like having one asthma attack after the other . . . but she doesn't want to have genetic testing. She doesn't like to go to doctors. I told her to do it, but she doesn't listen to me anymore. Yes! It makes me sad. I don't have a family of my own and my sister treats me like a nobody. I want to be treated with respect . . . not because I'm sick, you have to treat me like, "Oh this poor man." I hate that! Besides, this [economic problem] makes everything sadder. Before [while working] I was able to put my hand in my pocket and they [mother and sisters] had anything they needed. They did not need to ask; if I saw they needed something I was there for them. I didn't want them to suffer any deprivation. But now I can't do anything. The money I get from disability is not even enough for me and my mother, much less to help others . . .

In comparing Carlos's and his sister's narratives, we saw that Maria appeared to be far more accepting of her situation. But like her brother, Maria's greatest concern was also the impact of her illness on family relations.

Maria: Sometimes Carlos is angry . . . and other days I see him depressed. I tell my brother we have to accept [reality] and [for myself] I'm thankful that it is now when I am experiencing the worsening symptoms and not when my children totally depended on me . . .

As time passed, Carlos continued to try to make sense of the genetic diagnosis.

Carlos: Silvia doesn't want to have [genetic testing] because she doesn't believe [it is genetic] and I don't blame her. What I don't understand is where we got it [from]. [The doctors] said they saw in the tests that it is hereditary ... but why? My parents were always well. Then I began to think, it could be other things. We were breathing pesticides [in Mexico] when we were in the fields. I worked in the fields many years and the owner of the farm used to fumigate all the time. My sisters didn't work in the fields but our home was just a few blocks away. So they could have inhaled the same pesticides ... and this may be why we got [the symptoms] later [in life], because none of us were born with defects. My mother says we were beautiful children.

Maria was far less preoccupied than Carlos with finding a cause for their medical problems. But with the passage of time, like both Carlos and Eduarda, she continued to worry about the impact of their shared illness on family dynamics and family functioning.

Maria: My sister [Silvia] didn't have the genetic test because after so many years [of treatment], she's lost faith in doctors. It's not lack of respect for him, as Carlos says. But she did say to me, "Why pay attention to him, he follows doctors' [advice] like a little lamb, and see what he gets? Nothing! My problems [symptoms] are worse than his and yours," she said, "but I can handle them better without putting so much garbage [pharmaceuticals] in my body." [And] she and I have come to accept that we won't be able to do things as before. Silvia thinks that Carlos does not accept that [reality] and this is why he suffers the most ... but she loves him and feels sorry for him ... My mother also suffers because Silvia and Carlos have become distant ... we were always very close.

During our final conversations with the Estrada family, each continued to focus on a distinct set of concerns. Those of Carlos revolved around the consequences of his shrinking economic options, and he told us he was considering returning to Mexico.

Carlos: In Mexico everything is more natural and cheaper ... and there are still places where you could live with a clean sky [without pollution]. I've been thinking that it would be nice to move there. It may help us feel better because the medicines my doctor prescribed in the last year are just not helping me at all. I really don't know what I should do next ... Here [in the States] everything is so expensive. It's very difficult to live off a Social Security check, with all the drugs and all of that ... In Mexico, drugs cost less and if I live there with money from here, [it] will be easier. Money is everything.

Carlos's mood began to improve with the prospect of a new long-term life plan in Mexico, and he became more socially engaged. Eduarda's sense of equanimity also began to be restored.

Eduarda: These days I'm feeling a lot better because Carlos looks much happier ... His health hasn't changed; in fact the other day, he had an accident on his way to his English class. It wasn't serious: he lost his balance but didn't actually fall down. But he's so happy that his teacher gave him an A for the semester!

Although Maria cautiously endorsed Carlos's plan to migrate as a potentially viable response to his worsening health and declining economic options, she was not fully convinced that his plan was a realistic one.

Maria: My brother said he doesn't know what to do now [after the positive test result] ... I told him we have to keep fighting. He was very depressed [with the genetic diagnosis]. Last week he finally seemed better and he told me that he would like to move back to Mexico if he could get the disability checks sent there. He says that life there is cheaper and he thinks he could convince my children to go with him. Carlos thinks he could help his nephews get a good education there, where it's more affordable. I don't know ... that's a dream ... it's *his* dream ...

Discussion

A number of themes emerge from these narrative accounts of family members facing the effects of chronic genetic neurodegenerative disease, but here we will develop just three: the value of a family systems conceptual approach for understanding the experiences of families with genetic disease; the meaning of a genetic diagnosis to them; and the gendered experience that the stigma of genetic disease had for the Estrada family.

Family systems conceptual framework

A contextual approach derived from family systems theory proved fruitful for understanding the Estrada family's experiences with a chronic and stigmatizing degenerative neurological disorder in which several family members were affected. We will further develop some of these insights in Chapter 5, which focuses on family members caring for neurodegenerative patients. Our primary objective here, however, has been to explicate some of the ways that the illness experiences of one family member can influence those of others, and in addition, transform broader interactional dynamics within a larger family group.

We showed how adding Eduarda's and Maria's narratives to Carlos's enriched our understanding of the obstacles the three children endured growing up in a small town, facing other children's taunts, neighbors' gossip, social marginalization, and other forms of cruelty. Their narratives also highlighted some of the convergent and divergent ways that children in the same family may accommodate to a serious, shared ongoing medical problem. In particular, their accounts reveal some of the ways each sibling's unique experiences and adaptations affected the family as a whole.

Insights about broader family dynamics can also be drawn from this material. A fundamental feature of life in families where children are disabled from childhood is that patterns of interaction formed in childhood may be perpetuated throughout adult life. Such children may never truly "grow up," leave home, or form their own families. Already overprotective parents may continue to feel overwhelmingly responsible for their adult children's welfare. In some families, children are so impaired from an early age that they never really function as adults; in others, there is a progressively worsening condition and an arc-shaped pattern: the child becomes independent for a while, only to revert to dependency as the disability advances. With Carlos and his mother, Eduarda, we saw features of both patterns.

For the Estrada siblings, the positive genetic test result had ramifications beyond the diagnostic information it provided. It moved Carlos closer to understanding – and, perhaps, accepting what the future held in store for him. While not the most severely impaired of the three siblings, his physical limitations and sense of stigma had kept him from marrying and having a family of his own. Yet these same factors impelled him to become a successful provider and earned from his mother and sisters the respect customarily accorded the head of a household; they were also central to his core sense of self-worth. As he explained it, "The important thing is that in one way or another, I always managed to take care of my family."

This family dynamic remained stable as long as Carlos was producing income. But losing his last job, which was full time, permanent, and with benefits, precipitated a spiral downward. In addition to the obvious economic consequences, job loss represented emasculation. Throughout our conversations, particularly the latter ones, he recounted insults and perceived slights in a variety of situations, ranging from his embarrassment that "as a man" he could not even pick up the check when we invited him for coffee, to the fact that he could no longer provide his family with money they needed.

The genetic diagnosis made things worse for him. He characterized this event as ". . . the beginning of the end" and emphasized his feelings of frustration and concern "because things [had] changed." Here, the "things" he referred to were not economic, but mostly social and psychological: he blamed the diagnosis for the new distance between him and his younger sister and his growing wish to be left alone.

The variable meaning of a genetic diagnosis

Despite their shared medical histories, it was not surprising to learn that the offer of genetic testing had very different meanings for each of the three siblings (cf. Forrest *et al.* 2003; Van Riper 2005; Van Riper and McKinnon 2004). But perhaps even more interesting, once Maria and Carlos had the results, neither seized upon a simple genetic explanation as the likely source of their medical problems. Maria thought that "other things could be going on" and Carlos focused on their earlier pesticide exposure.

With her own children nearly grown but still asymptomatic, and the prospect of grandchildren not far off, Maria had the most at stake in knowing whether or not her

problems were genetic. Despite her fears in confirming what she had long suspected, she availed herself of the opportunity to discover whether indeed her problem was inherited. Her disappointment with the genetic diagnosis was balanced by
an enormous sense of relief because her children were already grown, making it
easier to face her uncertain future. She further valued the genetic diagnosis as
providing proof, especially to her husband's side of the family, that her inability to
fulfill certain family obligations over the years was due to "real" and not imagined
disability.

Maria's perspective contrasted diametrically with Silvia's. Although she had
heard as a child that her problems were inherited, Silvia had gone on to endure years
of ineffective medical treatments. Recently married, and still childless, she was
noncommittal about her plans to reproduce. She was firm, however, in wanting
nothing to do with genetic testing and steadfastly refused to acknowledge that a
chromosomal defect was the source of the family's medical problems. She faulted
her brother for uncritically accepting the medical explanation and being overly
submissive to doctors, since in her view, all his efforts had been futile.

Carlos manifested both these perspectives. At first he was pleased to finally be
given a reason for his worsening symptoms and hopeful this information would
enable doctors to offer him and his sisters more effective treatments. But after
months without seeing any improvement from his new medicines, he grew disillu-
sioned and began once again to search for other explanations. As time went on,
Carlos became even more convinced that environmental factors had contributed to,
if not actually caused his disease and he began to think about relocating to Mexico
taking along as much of his family as would go with him. He figured that his disability payments would afford them a better standard of living there, and that he
could find them a place to live in a less toxic environment. These changes would
enable him to reestablish himself as head of the family.

Carlos's plan offers interesting other parallels with Enrique Silvestre's in
Chapter 3. Both rurally-raised immigrant males (albeit from different social class
backgrounds), both sought to accommodate to their impending disability by returning to a rural setting in the land of their birth. But where Enrique had the resources
and actually managed to carry out his plan, the status of Carlos's "dream" was still
unclear at the time of our last encounter.

Stigma and genetic disease

The stigma linked to what Irving Goffman famously characterized as "spoiled identity" was evident in the Estrada family's experiences (Goffman 1963). Stigma
refers to regarding an individual as undesirable and rejecting that person because
they manifest attributes, behavior, or other characteristics deemed socially undesirable or unacceptable. The sense of stigma associated with a genetic diagnosis figured in both Maria's and Carlos's narratives, but in distinctly different ways. Maria
was optimistic that the genetic diagnosis would provide definitive proof that their
condition was real, not invented (Armstrong, Michie, and Marteau 1998). To her
mind, a genetic diagnosis, indeed *any* diagnosis, would offer relief and reassurance

"because everyone will see, once and for all, that we're not lying" (*porque todos verán que no estamos engañándolos*).   impact on relationship w/others-

Carlos experienced his SMA as more globally stigmatizing than either of his sisters. He told us that he never married because his once potential mother-in-law had disdained him for his disability, and that he never pursued other girlfriends for the same reason. As his health continued to deteriorate, Carlos's depression, anger, and hypersensitivity may have been a reaction to these and similar stigmatizing social experiences, as much as to economic ones. Throughout the period of our acquaintance, we noticed that he fought hard to overcome them, a process we call "preservation of dignity" (*defensa de la dignidad*). We saw this manifested in many ways: the enormous discomfort evoked by the prospect of receiving long-term disability payments from the government; telling us he would rather walk to the bus stop than accept our offer of a ride; refusing seats on the bus offered by other passengers; anger at clinicians he found patronizing ("Do [the doctors] think I'm stupid [and that] because I'm sick I'm unable to understand?"). For Carlos, like for many other study participants including Enrique, what seemed most important was that they not be pitied. He explained, "What's hardest for me, what's made me suffer the most, more than not being able to walk, is when people pity me; that people think, 'Poor thing!' . . . I want them to say, 'Look how well he does!' I really like going to the [English] classes because the teacher says to me, 'See how well you speak!'"

Betsy Fife and Eric Wright's (2000) framework for assessing the effects of stigma on one's sense of self worth and identity is useful for understanding the diverse features of Carlos's and Maria's stigmatization experiences. These researchers sought to determine whether people with different types of illness might experience stigma differently. To do so, they compared patients with HIV/AIDS and cancer along four hypothesized dimensions of perceived stigmatization: social rejection, financial insecurity, internalized shame, and social isolation. They found that while stigma was a major force in the lives of both groups, the HIV/AIDS patients had significantly higher scores on all four measures. Although Fife and Wright's study populations contained both women and men, they did not examine whether the effects of stigma might be gendered. However such a pattern was very clear in our own study population.

Men's experiences of stigmatization manifested in financial insecurity, social rejection, and social isolation, while women's experiences more explicitly revolved around internalized shame. Like Carlos, other male study participants repeatedly referred to frustrations and fears associated with financial insecurity as a consequence of their illness, and they talked openly about social rejection, particularly at work and with female partners. Also, like Carlos, other male study participants seemed to have isolated themselves socially more than the women did, perhaps to protect themselves from future rejections. As Garry Aguirre, another study participant, explained, "I decided to be alone. That's better than being with people who feel sorry for me. [And now] I need to go to the next level; I need to live in solitude, which is not the same as living alone." Enrique Silvestre was seeking a similar accommodation.

The female study participants' stigmatization experiences tended to mirror Maria's, who had lived for years haunted by feelings of shame. Like her, other women were fearful that relatives, friends, associates, or neighbors regarded them as liars who were exaggerating their symptoms to gain love or attention, or manipulators who used their illness to avoid responsibilities. Others were shamed by the thought that bosses or co-workers would discover they could no longer perform their job responsibilities. While a few women, like Liz Morgan in Chapter 1, eventually adopted a more "male" approach and abandoned social interaction entirely, most women's responses were more socially oriented, as illustrated by Ana Almendra in Chapter 2, who became closer to her mother. Women like these sought to come to terms with feelings of shame by consulting psychologists or seeking support of friends and family. *coping strategies*

The Estrada family's narratives illuminate the complex experience of a family with a chronic genetic disease. We examined ways in which their lives were transformed once they had proof that their symptoms were genetic in origin. While such a diagnosis has typically been seen in a negative light because of its stigmatizing potential and implications for the health of other family members, we showed that for individuals already ill, a genetic diagnosis can be legitimizing, and even liberating, providing a long-sought explanation for their symptoms. Yet in and of itself, a definitive genetic diagnosis did little to restore meaning or improve future outlook for the Estrada siblings. Although knowing the origin of their symptoms alleviated certain doubts, it also precipitated grave new ones, along with the need for new strategies to cope with the many uncertainties of the journey ahead.

Carlos
maria

Part III

Caregivers

Parts I and II considered patients who were struggling while living with the manifestations of neurodegenerative disease. We examined the processes through which they sought to obtain accurate diagnoses and analyzed some of the strategies they created to reconstruct their lives after their diagnoses predicted only bleak futures. Now we turn to some of the family caregivers and clinicians who cared for those patients. In considering their experiences and perspectives, we focus particularly on the meaning and use of genetic diagnoses.

Chapter 5 focuses on family caregivers. We explore the range of interactional dynamics we observed between patients and relatives who provided day-to-day care as well as assisted patients in their quests for diagnostic information and treatment. We also consider the specific types of strategies caregivers devised to manage their relatives' emotional and physical needs. We offer four dyads that illustrate a continuum of approaches the family caregivers in our study developed to meet patients' expectations along with their efforts to adapt to their new lives, which often included intensified fears of dependency on others. We reveal how genetic diagnoses were employed in these adaptational processes. As in Chapter 4, a family systems theoretical framework, which posits that major life stresses such as chronic illness affect not just the individual but the entire family, is employed to explicate how progressive neurodegenerative diseases can profoundly alter all aspects of communication and broader interaction among relatives.

In Chapter 6 we look at the neurologists who cared for the patients in our investigation. Their stories reveal the distinct nature of their frustrations and concerns about the limitations of biomedicine, and the efforts they made to help patients and families deal with the difficult realities of trying to live with incurable neurodegenerative diseases. The clinicians' narratives, along with our systematic observations of their interactions with patients and relatives during clinical encounters, also cast light on some of the challenges these doctors faced in their efforts to keep hope alive in the face of failed treatments. It is in this regard that we find the perspectives of the neurologists most meaningful for understanding the patients' and family caregivers' experiences, as these clinicians decided whether, when, and how a genetic diagnosis would or would not be relevant to them.

5 Maintaining hope and independence in the face of despair

In earlier chapters we focused on patients' experiences in living with progressive movement disorder symptoms and analyzed some of the processes by which they sought to come to terms with their neurodegenerative diseases. We paid special attention to the variable significance of a genetic diagnosis in their adaptational processes.

We saw that family caregivers were important in patients' adaptations to their new and altered lives in varying ways and to differing degrees (Rankin and Weekes 2000). This chapter focuses on 47 family caregivers who participated in our study to offer a more nuanced perspective on patients' experiences and the nature of their efforts to adapt.[1] We will examine the meaning of the care the relatives provided, the impact of their care giving activities on patients' identity and sense of wellbeing, and, in these contexts, the actual or potential significance of information derived from genetic testing (Bharadwaj 2002; Lock 2008).

As mentioned before, like most family caregivers worldwide (Burgess and D'agincourt-Canning 2001; D'agincourt-Canning 2001; Durán 2003), those in our study were overwhelming female and mostly middle aged, and generally younger than the patients. Children (12 daughters, 6 sons) and others in the descending generation (4 nieces, 1 goddaughter, 1 daughter-in-law) constituted the largest proportion, followed by spouses (7 wives, 4 husbands), siblings (6 sisters, 1 sister-in-law), and parents (5 mothers).

As is the case for most patients throughout the world who are suffering from the effects of chronic medical conditions, family members provided "the first line of support" for most patients in this investigation (Kane, Priester, and Totten 2005: 38). We further found that for many, relatives were the *only* line of support. Caregiver tasks involved helping with personal care (e.g. bathing, dressing, etc.), providing emotional support and companionship, managing medications, performing household tasks (e.g. meal preparation, housework, bill paying, etc.), coordinating medical care, offering transportation, and helping with decisions about diagnosis and treatment options. The needs of individual patients were, of course, variable and changed over time. Interestingly, and consistent with other research on the subject, for the most part we found no direct correlation between degree of disease progression and amount of family involvement (Rankin and Weekes 2000).

Families are necessarily invariably affected by the chronic illness of a member in ways that extend beyond simply reallocating or reconceptualizing accustomed roles and responsibilities. Accordingly, as in Chapter 4, we will again draw upon the family systems theoretical framework to analyze some of the consequences of chronic illness for family units. Also as before, our starting assumption is that families are systems of patterned reciprocal relationships, and that chronic illness affects the entire family, not just the individual. Joan Patterson and Ann Garwick have identified the relevant dimensions and dynamics of these processes:

> The reciprocal impacts between illness, individual development and family functioning continue dynamically in a circular pattern of effects over time . . . [and are] influenced by the meanings families attribute to their situation as well as to their own identity as a family unit and to their view of the world.
>
> (Patterson and Garwick 1994:131)

Family systems frameworks, typically used in research on families with young children, can, as we saw in Chapter 4, be fruitfully extended to families with chronically ill adults to ascertain the reciprocal impacts of chronic, and in these cases genetically caused, illnesses.

In seeking to understand these reciprocal and mutually reinforcing processes, we noticed interesting variability in the ways that caregivers and patients interacted during medical encounters, often apparent from the moment of our first introductions. For instance, some relatives went out of their way to make the medical consultation as comfortable as possible for the patient, while others acted as if accompanying the patient was an imposition or burden. We also noticed that patients who were treated by family caregivers with warmth and respect, and who enjoyed more autonomy during the medical consultations, tended to be more interested in participating in our research. Through conversations with patients and family caregivers we observed that some care giving approaches seemed more effective at preserving patients' independence, which, for many, was of utmost importance. This notion is consistent with Gay Becker's view that patients who are more independent more easily adapt to the challenges created by their illness and they experience a greater sense of wellbeing (Becker 1997).

As we did in earlier chapters, we employed an inductive analytical process to operationalize our criteria for effective care (Patton 2002). During an informal conversation in the waiting room of a general neurology clinic, we were struck by the simplicity and astuteness of the definition of effective care volunteered by Luis Collado, a paid, non-family caregiver for one of the patients we were recruiting:

> First and most importantly, it's a job that we must want to do. It's not something that we should be sent to do. It's like love; we can't be forced to love another person. But we must expect that if caregivers do not "love" their patients, they will at least respect them. Second, we need to keep in mind that we're caring for a person: body and soul . . . [Unfortunately] the soul is often

forgotten because it doesn't show symptoms, but both need to be equally nourished.

Using Collado's definition, we identified two key dimensions of effective care: the caregiver's attitude toward their care giving responsibilities, and the extent to which the caregiver appeared supportive of patients' own goals. Reviewing our interview and observational data for the 47 patient–family caregiver dyads with the above dimensions in mind yielded four distinct caregiver approaches. We were further fascinated, although perhaps we should not have been, to find that the different caregiver approaches were associated with distinctly different patient wellbeing outcomes, as follows:

Facilitative (n = 25; 53.2 percent)
  Caregiver freely embraced role
  Caregiver provided patient unconditional support and freedom (within the patient's physical limitations)
  Patient's level of wellbeing high; patient is engaged

"Shadow" (n = 6; 12.8 percent)
  Caregiver freely embraced role
  Caregiver offered patient unconditional support but limited the patient's freedom
  Patient's level of wellbeing low; patient is unengaged

Ambivalent (n = 12; 25.5 percent)
  Caregiver acted with ambivalence towards his/her role
  Caregiver offered interventional support and limited patient's freedom
  Patient's level of wellbeing low; patient is unengaged

Unsupportive (n = 4; 8.5 percent)
  Caregiver was obliged to provide care, lacked own independent desire to do so
  Caregiver offered only formal care and limited the patient's freedom to an extreme extent
  Patient's level of wellbeing extremely low; patient is unengaged

Further on we offer illustrative examples of the four types of patient–family caregiver dyads and their associated dynamics. In situations where patients told us that they received help from multiple family caregivers, we sought to recruit the relative who accompanied the patient to the neurogenetics consultation where the initial patient recruitment occurred, unless we determined that a different relative was more consistently and extensively involved in the patient's care. Also, please note that these four "ideal" types do not, of course, reflect the precise characteristics of every actual relationship between a neurodegenerative patient and the patient's primary family caregiver, but rather reflect our attempt to explicate the broad features of the interactional dynamics we observed within the contexts of an actual or potential impact of a genetic diagnosis. Finally, whether it is, in fact, right that family members be expected to assume major care giving responsibilities for relatives with chronic and deteriorating conditions is a much larger question of societal priorities and social policy.

The four patient–caregiver dyads

Facilitative approach

Mary Solomon, age 52, employed a facilitative approach in caring for her brother Roland Pilgrim, a 57-year-old Anglo man with Huntington's disease. As adults, the siblings had grown apart after Roland moved to Chicago to pursue a career as a jazz clarinetist, and their contact was primarily limited to the occasional holiday phone call. Over time, as his symptoms worsened, it became harder, and then impossible for Roland to get work as a musician. For a while he managed to support himself as a taxi driver but eventually his memory became too impaired for him to continue driving. Homeless, Roland drifted back to his home state, and lived on the streets for four years. Eventually he was arrested for vagrancy and called Mary to see if she would bail him out of jail.

Mary was relieved and happy to be back in contact with Roland, and she fervidly wanted him to move into her home. At first, Mary's husband was not at all keen on the prospect and the couple spent considerable time and effort trying to reach an accord. In the end they agreed that they would invite Roland to come to live with them, and once they had reached that consensus, Mary was pleased to discover that her own relationship with her husband improved markedly. To their surprise, Roland turned down their offer, saying he preferred to remain independent and on his own. Mary then set about finding a residential facility near her home that would accept Roland's state disability benefits. The two remained in close and frequent contact. Mary helped Roland with medical and other daily needs and held Roland's power of attorney, which, she explained, she would use only when and if her brother became too impaired to make his own medical decisions.

Mary's care giving activities extended far beyond helping her brother meet his everyday needs. Once he was no longer homeless, Roland wanted to start playing music again and together they looked for groups of musicians that might welcome him. She drove him to auditions until they found one that seemed congenial and helped him establish a practice schedule. We are convinced that Mary's efforts to enable Roland to continue to enjoy performing, and even to improve his skills, were extremely important to the positive self-image in Roland that we observed. For example, in the course of our getting to know the siblings, at one point in a conversation, Roland drew himself to his full posture and told us, "It's nice to see that I still got it [when I play jazz]."

Mary was very proud of her brother and of how much he had achieved despite his advancing H.D. She believed he had managed to escape from homelessness by virtue of his determination "to keep it going"; and that doing so while remaining independent made his accomplishment all the more remarkable: "He worked hard to maintain his free spirit despite his physical deterioration," she told us, adding, "All the obstacles he encountered still didn't stop him from developing his musical talents."

Mary was modest about her own efforts on her brother's behalf, saying it was "the normal thing to do" and that "it couldn't be done in any other way." She bore the burdens of her responsibility lightly. Asked, for instance, whether she would want any remuneration for her efforts, she looked askance: "I'm already compensated. It feels good to help those who suffer and I hope somebody will take care of me if I, in turn, need help in the future." (She indicated, however, that she does not expect to develop Huntington's disease, having tested negative for the gene.)

Mary's own life had also been transformed through caring for her brother. She told us that Roland's H.D. diagnosis prompted her to embark on "a mission" to help other H.D. patients and their families. She was long acquainted with and knowledgeable about the disease because of the many years she had spent helping care for her grandfather and her mother, who both suffered from it. During the time we were in contact, she was in the process of creating a website to educate and inform others that genetic illnesses may "disrupt the life of a family, but not necessarily break it." During the period of our acquaintance, these activities had begun to impinge upon the time she could devote to her job as a graphic designer and she resolved to seek paid employment in a new area that would "give [her] more satisfaction, like an H.D. advocate, social worker, or counselor."

Our observations of interactions between Roland and Mary during two consultations at a neurogenetics specialty clinic showed marked reciprocal support and appreciation. They joked and bantered with one another while waiting for the doctors and seemed to enjoy each other's company. Mary demonstrated extraordinary patience by allowing her brother to remain in charge of clinical encounters despite his difficulties in talking with clinicians. She sat quietly while he laboriously filled out medical forms and decided about follow up appointment dates. She gave Ronald the opportunity to explain, in his own time and words, his concerns about his symptoms and to decide what clinical suggestions he felt most comfortable with and most able to follow. She answered questions only when directly asked. She regularly offered warm, encouraging looks or smiles that seemed to convey a shared sense of brother-sister understanding when Roland appeared troubled by questions asked by clinicians. On one occasion, when he was having trouble remembering the name of one of his medications, she said reassuringly, "Don't worry; my memory's worse than yours!" Roland, on the other hand, frequently elicited Mary's opinion and thanked her by patting her hand. When, in his presence, she mentioned her desire to pursue a career as a social worker or H.D. advocate, he enthusiastically endorsed her plan: "She will be the best!"

"Shadow" approach

Anisha Washington was a 44-year-old African American woman from a working-class background who, in striving to maintain her ailing husband's public persona as a respected deacon of his church, inadvertently sacrificed his sense of self-mastery and independence. Anisha, the mother of three adult children, was married to her second husband, John Washington, age 50. When we met the couple, John's health was deteriorating as a consequence of a neurodegenerative disease of undetermined origin; the most recent diagnosis the couple had been given was neurosarcoidosis, a central nervous system disorder. John had been employed as a restaurant manager until he could no longer perform his required tasks. With her husband's health declining, Anisha increasingly became the family's main bread-winner, taking on additional work in the fields of cosmetology and catering. When we met them, the couple was under extreme economic stress, as John's growing impairment required Anisha to devote an ever-increasing amount of time to his care. Anisha's three sons had temporarily moved back home to help make ends meet. Anisha also had an important decision to make: whether or not to accept John's brother's invitation for the couple to move to Detroit to live with him, a solution for which she had little enthusiasm: "Leaving my church and my children would break my heart," she gravely explained.

We were introduced to John and Anisha at the general neurology clinic of a large public teaching hospital. John had been admitted to the psychiatric unit a few days earlier because of extreme aggressive outbursts and talk of suicide. The attending psychiatrist felt that John would benefit from a neurological evaluation. It was during this evaluation that we met the couple. We learned that John first experienced balance problems ten years earlier, but they did not interfere with his ability to work or with other aspects of his daily life. However, four years ago, John crashed his truck and smashed his skull against the windshield. Soon after that, his memory deteriorated and he lost the ability to walk. Although those symptoms were initially brought under control, they returned permanently six months later.

We learned from Anisha that although the couple was most interested in stopping the advance of John's symptoms, they also wanted a clearer idea about their cause and they wondered whether a genetic test could provide an answer. Anisha seemed unsure about John's previous diagnosis (at one point referring to it as "East Coast Disease") but was also visibly uncomfortable directly asking Dr Jackson, the attending physician, about the diagnosis. When that clinician left the room Anisha turned to Dr Hamedan, a neurology resident, to ask whether he thought her husband's problem could be hereditary. Dr Hamedan said that was possible since neurosarcoidosis occurs much more frequently in African Americans than in other groups. The doctor went on to explain that they could not give the couple a definitive answer to Anisha's question because the genes involved in the neurosarcoidosis had not yet been identified and there were no genetic tests to diagnose the condition.

Dr Hamedan left the consulting room but returned a short time later to report that he had consulted with a neurogenetics specialist and that there might, indeed, be some meaningful genetic tests for her husband. Although Anisha said she had already talked with members of John's family to determine if anyone had similar symptoms, and was told they did not, she seized on Dr Hamedan's suggestion, not so much for John, she explained, who had no biological offspring, but for John's brother and brother's children. She later told us: "My brother-in-law was so kind; he wants us to move into his home and help me care for John. I'd like to be able to tell him that John's problems are not genetic, so he'll have peace of mind for himself and his daughters. And if we have bad news, at least they would be better prepared."

Jim Werner, one of Anisha's sons, also accompanied his mother and stepfather to the neurology consultation. When we explained to him that participating in our study would involve at least one extended private conversation with his mother and his stepfather, Jim cautioned us not to expect too much from John. "Interviewing my father would be hard," he explained. "He is very ill. But my mother can help you, she's my father's shadow." In fact, Jim underestimated his stepfather's ability to communicate and we were able to learn quite a bit from him directly. Moreover, being able to talk with both Anisha and John enabled us to better understand the multiple meanings of Jim's shadow metaphor.

Anisha's description of her current relationship with John simultaneously underscored the physical costs and emotional contradictions that can be involved in providing long-term care to a family member with a neurodegenerative disease:

> Taking care of [John] is a blessing because he came into my life and helped my children and me. So now it's not a problem doing it for him. It hurts. I don't like to see him like this . . . It's kind of hard sometimes when my sons are not around, or when I get sick. But I enjoy every minute of it because he was a good man to me and my family. My kids' father was an abusive man. And when John came into our life, he was like a lifesaver, and I will never forget that. Right now he's like a little baby, but I don't mind . . . I don't care how hard it gets . . . I will still take care of him.

In fact, John's health had deteriorated to such an extent that he could no longer attend to his own basic needs and required help walking, eating, dressing, and bathing. But the toll of John's illness on Anisha went beyond the loss of a beloved husband and father. "The thing that really, really hurts me," said Anisha, "is that he'd lose his place in church. He is a special man and he gives advice even to our pastor. I'm afraid people won't come to us for help anymore. So I've been helping him do this job too." To clarify this last comment, she later explained:

> John is and always has been a good counselor. Now, when people come to us for advice, I tell them, "He's tired, but we'll think about this and we'll get back to you and we'll pray for you." And at night, when we're alone relax[ing], I ask him questions and he answers me, not in so many words, but I understand what he is telling me. [I know] what he is thinking. Then the next day I'll call and say, "John wants you to know . . . so and so."

We see, then, that John's illness transformed Anisha not only into a full time caregiver and the family breadwinner, but also, into the "shadow" role of informal church leader by covertly standing in for him as pastoral counselor. We believe that in doing so, Anisha managed to continue to project onto the world the image of John that she desperately wanted to remain intact. She reported receiving a deep sense of satisfaction from this approach: just as caring for John had enabled Anisha to repay her debt to him, helping parishioners allowed her to acknowledge her gratitude for the economic support they provided her family as John's symptoms worsened. In the month prior to our meeting, among other gifts they received from fellow parishioners was an automobile with the insurance, gas, and maintenance expenses fully covered.

Yet, as meaningful as Anisha's solution to John's deteriorating condition may have been for Anisha, and possibly for their fellow parishioners, the unintended and unfortunate consequence was that John's own voice was silenced. During our observations of the couple's interactions at two neurology consultations, and a couple of visits to their church and home, we saw that not only did Anisha become John's shadow, taking over his previous roles, but that John had become Anisha's shadow as well, as he relinquished his roles and became beholden to her. Over the course of the eight months we were in contact, we saw him become increasingly distant and progressively less communicative. In the few chats we had near the end of our acquaintance, he expressed concerns about Anisha's overwhelming responsibilities and his fear that she herself might become ill. One afternoon, he went further to confess that having Anisha doing "everything" for him had become too much to bear – and he was seriously considering accepting his brother's invitation to move to Detroit.

Ambivalent approach

Jessica Marks was a 42-year-old married Jewish American woman from an affluent neighborhood who made her living in the arts. We met in the waiting room of a neurogenetics specialty clinic where she had accompanied her brother, Dylan Kasden. Dylan, 49, had lived for years in a remote rural area but at his mother's urging had come back home for a neurogenetics evaluation. The family was seeking a diagnosis for Dylan's increasing difficulties with walking, balance, and coordination. Dylan lived alone, but relied, sometimes reluctantly, on his mother, sister, and a stepdaughter for help with things he could no longer manage (e.g. driving, domestic chores). In this regard, Dylan was similar to almost 20 percent of patients in this study who received help from multiple caregivers. As earlier indicated, in the event of multiple caregivers, we would preferentially attempt to recruit the one who had accompanied the patient to the neurology consultation. Accordingly we focused on Jessica and the relationship between the two siblings.

Jessica's ambivalence about helping her brother was evident from nearly the moment we met. She explained that she had accompanied Dylan not of her own volition but at their mother's request, adding "I needed to re-schedule an important meeting with my London agent." She appeared tense and unhappy while they waited to see the specialist and complained several times about the long wait. Her mood lightened and she became more cooperative once she and Dylan began filling out medical history forms, and she offered to call their mother to ask for information that neither of the siblings could provide (i.e. the date of Dylan's first symptoms). After being ushered into the consultation room, Jessica continued to act solicitously toward Dylan, asking if he felt comfortable in his seat and later offering him a magazine to pass the time before the neurologist arrived.

Jessica's pattern of ambivalence continued once the doctors arrived. On the one hand, she seemed interested in helping her brother provide accurate and detailed information about his symptoms. Yet, whenever Dylan would begin to answer a question, she invariably interrupted to answer for him or to correct his reply. For instance, during the personal history intake, Dr Dordoni, the neurology resident, asked Dylan about the main changes he had experienced in the previous four years. Speaking a bit hesitatingly, he replied, "I don't know. I don't see any big changes." Jessica quickly contradicted him: "Dylan, please think! You have had changes. Give the doctor the M.R.I." As he handed a large envelope to the physician, Dylan countered, "Well other people see those changes, I don't." Jessica also ordered her brother to provide information about relatives she believed had similar symptoms ("Dylan, tell the doctor about the family") and to describe a job where he had been exposed to possible toxins that she believed could have triggered his movement disorder ("Dylan, tell the doctor about your work . . . the solvents . . ."). At the same time, she also sought to appear warm and caring by smiling profusely at the clinicians, repeatedly thanking them, and again offering to obtain additional information about other family members' medical histories and email it to the doctors.

Jessica's ambivalence toward helping her brother remained evident in our subsequent conversations, as the following interview excerpt reveals:

H.M.P.: Why did you want to attend [the neurogenetics consultation]?

Jessica: My mother couldn't come. He couldn't attend by himself. [Besides] you know, Dylan. . . . Well, I love him, but I have to say that Dylan is a very special person and my mother and I wanted to know what was going on with his problem and we wanted to know what [this clinic] could offer him [regarding diagnosis and treatment]. But if it weren't for you . . . that you pushed him to invite me [She is referring to the ethnographer having asked her, "Are you going to join us?" as Dylan was being ushered into the consultation room], I wouldn't be there.

H.M.P.: I didn't push him.

Jessica: Well, you were in favor; at least that's what I thought, in favor of me being present.

H.M.P.: Well, yes.

Jessica: And if I hadn't been there it would have been impossible to get any information from Dylan. He keeps everything to himself.

She also expressed irritation with how Dylan had acted during the neurogenetics evaluation: "My mother made all the efforts to get him here. We were at the best institution we could ask for and instead of answering promptly and precisely, he mumbles the first thing that comes into his mind."

Jessica's attitude toward her brother and how he was managing his illness and medical care can be better understood when viewed in the context of the family's history of interactional dynamics between a highly controlling mother and a passive-aggressive son: "Mother is domineering and Dylan," Jessica explained, "does not volunteer information because she would take his words and find something to criticize." This history framed Dylan's response to his family's efforts to help with his care.

Jessica herself was generally in agreement with their mother about how Dylan should be managing his illness and living his life. In turn, while Dylan's antipathy toward his mother ran deep but was not overt, his resentment toward his sister was much more open. Months after our first meeting, Dylan told us, "Now that I don't see [Jessica] so often and I don't get in those eternal discussions with her, I feel that my health has improved. I love my sister, but if I let her in, she interferes with my freedom." In fact, he refused to tell Jessica whether or not he had ultimately had genetic testing and asked us not to do so either. He remarked, "She was in favor of me getting tested and she may think I did it. Let her think whatever she pleases. I believe she wants me to be tested not for me but for her, since we share the same gene pool." Around the same time, Jessica commented, "[As for me] now I'm only his sister-driver. That's all. He doesn't call me. . . . Dylan will always be Dylan but my obligation as a sister has its limits. I don't call him either."

Ambivalence in caring for chronically ill patients is obviously not limited to family members, but caring for a relative can add uniquely complex issues. We saw in this example (and will again in the next) how a neurodegenerative disorder can impose additional pressures on already strained family relationships, which can be exacerbated all the more by the availability of genetic testing. Dylan's efforts to preserve his sense of personhood and shape his life on his own terms led him to distance himself from his mother and sister, caregivers he found overly interfering, choosing to rely more on his stepdaughter and a spiritual healer who he believed were better able to help him achieve his goals.

Unsupportive approach

Rita Thomas, a 30-year-old African American woman, lived in a working-class neighborhood and was employed as a clerk at a national department store. We were introduced in the waiting room of the general neurology clinic of an HMO by Rita's uncle, Edward Rogers, age 60. Edward had had a difficult employment history, which he attributed to advancing diabetes. Although for years he worked full-time as a truck driver, more recently he had only been able to find part-time work. His last job was as a parking lot attendant. At the time of his hospitalization following a seizure, which had left him unconscious for several minutes, Edward had been sharing an apartment with a roommate in a rundown inner city neighborhood. It was during this hospitalization that he first began to experience problems with gait, balance, and coordination. In fact, he could no longer walk unassisted and was using a wheelchair when we were first introduced at the general neurology clinic of a large public hospital. Edward had been referred to the clinic by a neurologist at his HMO who had found Edward's case puzzling and requested a neurogenetics specialty consultation in an effort to determine whether a hereditary form of ataxia could be causing his symptoms.

It was clear that Rita did not want to be with her uncle that morning. She explicitly told us that her mother and other relatives had impelled her to oversee his medical care. Like the previous example, this illustrates some of the consequences for both patient and caregiver when relatives with longstanding resentments, in this case sustained from generation to generation, feel obliged to come together when one of them falls seriously ill. In such cases, as we shall see, the prospect of a genetic diagnosis can add fuel to an already explosive situation. This example differs from the previous three in that we witnessed two distinct approaches to a patient's care – one by a paid professional and the other by a family member.

When we initially met Edward, he was accompanied by Luis Collado, a health-care professional who worked at the hospital where Edward had previously been treated. We immediately noted the warm relationship between the two men. They shared passion for sports, particularly basketball, and we learned that Luis had been encouraging Edward to write a column for the hospital newsletter about the current season. During the consultation, Luis showed his respect for Edward by only answering questions directed at him, by providing details about Edward's medical history only when Edward could not remember them, and by helping him in and out of his wheelchair during the examination. Luis, we believe, enabled Edward to remain in control of the consultation and to maintain his sense of dignity. During this consultation, Edward spoke by and for himself and only when he was unsure about the answer to a question did he ask Luis to intervene (e.g. the names of different medications he was taking).

The second consultation of Edward's that we were able to attend was at the HMO's outpatient facility with the neurologist who had initially referred Edward for a genetics evaluation. By this point, Luis had been transferred to a different facility and Edward's niece Rita accompanied him. Although only a few weeks had passed, Edward seemed vastly changed. He was silent during most of the consultation and answered questions with either gestures or monosyllabic replies. Rita, on the other hand, was outspoken in her unhappiness about the fact that she was obliged to be there on a day when she felt she should have been at work. Although the neurologist made a couple of attempts to redirect attention from Rita to Edward, she remained unrelenting in guiding the focus back to her.

Rita did not show any warmth or concern for her uncle throughout the consultation, nor did she help him to get in and out of his wheelchair, leaving it to the neurologist to assist him. She routinely answered questions directed toward Edward and controlled most of the conversation. At one point Rita flatly dismissed Dr Brown's opinion that the source of her uncle's problems could be genetic:

[I don't believe it.] He drank all his life! As did his father before him! My grandmother died because of her husband [Edward's father]; he made her suffer and she had a heart attack. His [father's] drinking put our family through hell!

Subsequent conversations with Rita added depth to our understanding of her attitudes and behavior. We learned that she cared for her uncle only out of love and loyalty to her mother, who herself was too ill to do so, but who very much wanted her brother's care overseen by a family member. Rita said: "I am not doing it for him [Edward], although I'm sorry for what he is going through. [I'm doing it] for my mother. . . . She loves her brother. . . . I don't want *her* to die [because of frustration or disappointment with my uncle] like my grandmother did."

We saw Edward's health continue to decline following that neurology consultation. After he was discharged from the hospital, Luis, who had been transferred to another facility, still made a point of visiting Edward from time to time. Sometimes he would be there when we stopped by to see Edward. In Luis's view, "Edward's spirit had been broken." He reported that Edward had lost interest in reading the sports magazines Luis still brought him and that he spent much more time sleeping. In addition, the seizures that had originally brought Edward to the hospital had increased dramatically in number and frequency, and his family was making plans to permanently move him to a nursing home. Could Edward's sharp deterioration have been linked to the fact that his sense of personhood and wellbeing were disrupted when he lost Luis's compassionate care and understanding and became much more dependent on his niece? While we do not wish to suggest that Edward's decline was due only to Rita's hostile approach, we do believe more favorable care giving circumstances might have produced less dramatic and devastating consequences.

Rita's deep-seated resentment toward her uncle, and other men in her family, led her to blame Edward for his medical problems. Doing so absolved Rita of the need to play a significant role in her uncle's care because in her view: "You harvest what you sow." Convinced that his illness was the result of a lifetime of hard drinking, she was opposed to continuing to search for a defective gene after the initial genetic tests proved inconclusive. Yet, other family dynamics hampered Rita's ability to single-handedly put a halt to more genetic testing. She told us that without proof that her uncle's ataxia was *not* genetic, Rita's mother would continue to worry that she, Rita, and other family members were all at risk for the same disease. Moreover, lack of a definitive diagnosis and the family's intention to move Edward out of his own apartment was forcing Rita to continue in a role she openly detested. Edward's adaptation manifested as even greater withdrawal from both his family and society at large.

Discussion

The family systems framework illuminated some of the ways that patients' chronic and progressive neurodegenerative disorders can affect not just sick individuals but other relatives, and how living with these types of diseases can intensify or transform larger patterns of family interaction. In these contexts we considered the actual or potential impact of a genetic diagnosis.

Maintaining independence proved fundamental to many patients' sense of wellbeing as they strove to remain in charge of their lives despite increasing impairment. But while the actual or projected loss in the ability to perform customary social roles might initially have devastating effects on self-esteem, the problem could be ameliorated if the patient managed to modify existing roles or create new ones (see also Burke and Reitzes 1981; Stryker and Burke 2000; Turner 1978). In different ways, Enrique's and Carlos's stories as told in Chapters 3 and 4 showed this quite clearly. And moreover, just as patients experienced shifts and "disruptions" in their identities as they sought to adjust to worsening symptoms (Ezzy 2000), larger family units might also be affected, especially primary caregivers like Liz's husband in Chapter 1, and Carlos's mother to a lesser extent, who experienced a dramatic reframing of their own lives as well (Ready *et al.* 2008; Stets and Burke 2000).

Mary Solomon and Ronald Pilgrim's case highlighted some of the ways in which a neurological disorder can transform the lives of both the patient and the larger family unit (Etchegary and Fowler 2008). When Mary wanted to take in her brother who was suffering from H.D., she knew she would need to first negotiate with her husband and then with her brother. But neither negotiation produced the outcome that Mary had anticipated: her relationship with her husband unexpectedly improved, and her brother turned down the invitation. This experience caused Mary to recognize that preserving her brother's independence would be of the utmost importance as his physical condition deteriorated. She acted to help support the aspects of his life that he most valued: his independence and ability to perform as a musician. At the same time, Mary recognized that she could use the knowledge and experience she had acquired in the course of caring for relatives with H.D. to help others beyond her own family. At the end of our acquaintance, Mary was in the process of abandoning a less satisfying career to search for work that she expected would be much more meaningful for her.

Anisha Washington approached her caregiver responsibilities with the same love and passion as Mary Solomon. But while Mary's sense of fulfillment seems to have come from accepting her brother as he was, Anisha was motivated by a wish to preserve John's former image (Stets 1995). One wonders, in fact, whose needs were being served when Anisha adopted the practice of standing in for John as pastoral counselor. Also, in contrast with Mary, who managed to successfully combine family caregiver and professional responsibilities, we saw that Anisha was finding it increasingly difficult to do so; over time, she, too, began to show signs of depression, a common response in individuals who care for sick relatives for long periods of time without being able to also take their own needs into account (Beckham and Giordano 1986).

Jessica Marks and Dylan Kasden's example reveals how historical family dynamics can come into play in the adult lives of family caregivers and chronically ill patients. We saw that while growing up, the siblings already felt oppressed by a very controlling mother, but that each adapted differently to the situation. Dylan worked hard to distance himself from his mother, eventually moving thousands of miles away from her and from his sister, who in many ways acted as their mother's surrogate. Dylan's illness and need for assistance propelled him back into their orbit, reigniting the relational tensions we observed: bitter disagreements over whether Dylan should undergo genetic testing and Jessica's ambivalence regarding her brother's general care.

Historical family dynamics were also at play in the case of Rita Thomas and her uncle, Edward Rogers. However, in their story, we learned about resentments that extended back generations and had physical as well as emotional consequences for the health of the larger family system. And while it was difficult to determine whether Jessica would have continued to help her brother had she not been wanting to please her mother, it seemed obvious that Rita would have had nothing to do with her uncle were it not for her other and more important ties to her own mother. And as in Dylan and Jessica's example, we saw how longstanding family conflicts were made manifest in disagreements among relatives over the use of genetic testing.

Our objective in this chapter has been to explore the variable impact of an actual or potential genetic diagnosis on the everyday lives of gravely ill patients and their families. We also considered the often profound – and sometimes transformational – ramifications of long-term care giving responsibilities for family caregivers. In the next, we consider the variable meaning and use of diagnoses derived from genetic testing by clinicians.

6   The neurologists' conundrum

Until now, we have focused on the experiences of patients living with diverse neurodegenerative diseases and family members who helped care for them. Hardest to endure for patients were the progressive threats to their identity that accompanied their deteriorating health. Those who managed to forge new or modified versions of earlier identities within the constraints of increasing infirmity adapted much more successfully than those who did not. We also saw that family caregivers could be crucial in helping or hindering their relatives' adaptations to the changing realities of these patients' lives.

To further round out this ethnographic study, we now turn our focus to the neurologists who helped administer these patients' care, highlighting the challenges they faced in treating them and trying to help them and their families maintain hope in the face of progressive impairment. Several will be familiar from earlier chapters. Examining our participating clinicians' attitudes towards genetic testing and their views about the significance of genetic factors in movement disorders in general, and in their own clinical practices in particular, will add to our understanding of the everyday life experiences of patients with neurodegenerative disease and the relatives who help with their care (Atkinson, Parsons, and Featherstone 2001). Excerpts from our observational data will further illuminate the meaning and use of genetic testing information for clinical neurologists who treat patients with movement disorder symptoms. In contrast to some of the other fields of medicine (Burke et al. 2002; Burke and Emery 2002; Emery et al. 1999; Hoop et al. 2008), there remains a dearth of information on this subject.

Background

The 13 neurologists who participated in our study included seven men and six women who ranged in age from 31 to 65 (mean = 47.7). Like the patient sample, most were immigrants: just five were U.S.-born while the remaining eight came from diverse parts of the globe. With the exception of one who held a master's degree in genetics, none had formal training in genetics beyond a course or two in college or medical school. Several said they kept up with advances in the field by reading or attending conferences.

The 13 doctors worked in the three types of practice settings that were described in some detail in the Introduction. Four were neurologists in private neighborhood practices that consisted mainly of low-income Spanish-speaking patients. In the following analyses, we refer to these doctors as "neighborhood neurologists." Four were based in either a large public hospital or a university outpatient general neurology or movement disorder clinics that catered to patients from diverse ethnic and social class backgrounds. We call these doctors "institution-based neurologists." The remaining five, whom we call "specialty clinic neurologists," worked in a public or a private research facility that evaluated and treated patients from varying socioeconomic and ethnic backgrounds suffering neurological disorders with a potential or actual genetic factor.

The amount of experience these neurologists had with genetic testing varied dramatically by practice setting (cf. Lazarus 1988; Lock 1995). The neighborhood neurologists reported that they seldom treated movement disorder patients whom they considered good candidates for genetic testing, and that they ordered genetic tests for no more than ten patients a year. Of our three groups of clinicians, they also reported the least comfort discussing genetics and genetic issues with patients and family members. When they felt that genetic testing might be indicated for a patient, they either sought advice from more knowledgeable colleagues or referred the patient elsewhere.

The institution-based neurologists saw a greater number of patients whom they regarded as candidates for genetic testing, in part because they received referrals from a large number of neighborhood doctors in the region. Still, they estimated the proportion of their movement disorder patient load for which genetic testing might be indicated at only about 5 percent. These neurologists, however, were far more comfortable with the subject of genetics than the neighborhood neurologists: they told us that talking with patients and their relatives about genetic issues associated with neurodegenerative diseases and ordering and interpreting the results of genetic tests posed no particular difficulties.

The specialty clinic neurologists indicated that most patients they treated were potential candidates for genetic testing (which was, after all, the designated purpose of their clinics). Like the institution-based neurologists, these doctors also felt comfortable discussing genetic issues with patients and family members and interpreting genetic test results.

Neurologists' views about genetic testing

The neurologists in all three types of practice settings were unanimous in the view that the recent rapid advances in genetics and genetic testing had great future potential for individuals and for society. This remark by Dr Samora, age 64 and native of South America, was typical:

> I constantly marvel at the advances in this area. I believe, but I really don't know, whether we'll see great benefits in our own lifetime. I also believe

genetic studies will continue to advance science and I'm hopeful that future generations will diagnose better and cure more quickly.

These clinicians' faith that society will one day reap tangible benefits from these scientific advances was tempered to some degree by the current reality. Dr Green,[1] a 52-year-old institution-based neurologist, explained that for doctors the field of medical genetics was still of limited clinical value and the existence of genetic testing could even have significant negative consequences for patients and members of their families.

> The drawbacks can be enormous. Identifying an abnormal gene that somebody carries that has a high penetrance or incomplete penetrance for a disease that we can't really treat or do anything about is, in a way, terrible information. I am going through this now with a family where one [relative] has a possible diagnosis of H.D., and the [others], quite frankly, don't want that [diagnosis] to be [confirmed]. It is actually an elderly woman who has the problem, and in the course of our discussion, you can just see in the room in the other family members, it's sort of just dawning on them that if she does in fact have H.D. – which they all say fervently is not the case – but if she did, then, my gosh – they're all at risk, their kids are at risk, their kid's kids and it just goes on and on! That's the down side of genetic testing, that it opens up a lot of anxiety and worry about one's future.

Dr King, the 55-year-old specialty clinic neurologist who we met in Chapters 1 and 2 expressed similar concerns about some of the larger ramifications of genetic testing, particularly for the larger family group, a theme we elaborated upon in Chapter 5. He observed:

> Being able to make a diagnosis of a genetic syndrome in a family . . . may open up a huge Pandora's box. . . . I know older parents at risk for Huntington's Disease, or symptomatic with a late onset milder form . . . who go and get genetic testing because their doctors said, "Well, maybe it's a rare form of Huntington's Disease," without discussing the implications of this information. And they get a positive test and they share it with the family, and all their adult children are now in a panic. A panic! If he was never tested and he never knew and nobody ever knew, it's kind of like the ostrich with their head in the ground. But I have seen adult children become quite angry with an older parent who elected to have testing done, which makes zero sense when you think about it. *Because if you have a risk to have this gene, not being tested is not going to take that risk away* . . . [emphasis in original]. You know, if it's quiet, nobody knows about it and the parent is never tested and nobody's the wiser: they've got [he simultaneously raised his index and middle fingers from both hands] "Parkinson's Disease," that's one thing. But the truth, although it's important will cause anxiety and depression. So even if they have no symptoms at all of Huntington's disease, they themselves may become anxious and depressed because of this knowledge.

Yet despite broad general agreement among the clinicians in our study as to the significance of genetic advances for the field of neurology, they differed widely in their perspectives on the current clinical significance of genetic testing for movement disorder patients. The neighborhood and institution-based neurologists told us that, for the most part, genetic advances were not yet very meaningful for movement disorder patients, but the two groups felt this way for different reasons. Institution-based Dr Green spelled out the pros and cons of genetic testing for his patients:

> Quite frankly, [genetic testing] has not had a huge impact [in my practice]. The big change came in the early '90s when the DNA test for H.D. became available. That was a distinct change in my practice, because so often these family histories are so hard to figure out: the father left home when the person was seven and they don't know what happened to him. And [genetic testing] makes the diagnosis more secure, and that is a diagnosis that one wants to be secure about. Otherwise I don't know if it has had a huge impact. There are other tests that are commercially available that I just don't order because they are not really of pragmatic value: testing for the Parkinson gene, [certain] autosomal recessive genes, the frequency is quite small. Why would I test them for that? Just to tell them that they have it? I don't really see the utility of that. So some of these other tests that are available, I just don't use, because I can't quite figure how that would change the management or care of my patients.

The neighborhood neurologists' views were similar to Dr Green's about the currently limited value of genetic testing for patients with movement disorder symptoms. For instance, Dr Larea, who was 55 and brought up in South America, said:

> I'm not 100 percent sure [about the value] but I believe there is one. Because I believe that the more knowledge one has, the easier it is to diagnose with more precision. And it could help to know in advance the prognosis, [for instance] when the person will deteriorate or remain stable. I believe all this could help *me* [to make plans about my job and my life if I myself had the disease]; but at this moment, it's not much help [for treating my patients, who are usually elderly and have scarce economic resources].

In addition to the limited clinical utility of genetic testing perceived by these neighborhood neurologists, they were faced with practical constraints, as Dr Samora explained:

> Economic realities must be taken into consideration. If I know that the patient wouldn't be eligible for free testing or if I think the patient has no means to pay [for genetic testing] I simply don't offer such a test . . . .

A second set of concerns raised by the neighborhood neurologists concerned the amount of effort they and their staff had to expend to make a successful referral. Dr Larea said:

For my poor patients, of course I can send them to the county hospital and it's a very good service. But it takes a lot of time, a lot of effort, a lot of energy, a lot of patience, to keep pushing, pushing, justifying . . . And if and when I finally succeed and get the referral approved, I don't know *how* or *if* genetic information finally benefits *that particular patient* who we decided to send for further tests [emphasis in original].

Dr Larea's response foreshadows the third set of considerations for these neighborhood neurologists: which patients should be given the opportunity to be offered genetic testing? For the most part, these clinicians were convinced that genetic information had no meaning in the lives of their low-income patients, offered no benefit to them, and, as shown earlier, could actually cause problems of their own. Dr Larea elaborated:

To whom do I offer genetic tests? We could say that I offer them primarily to those who ask for them. Like my colleague's relative, who was terrified because he wanted to get married and his fiancée wanted to have children but there had been a case of Huntington's in a close relative and this young man didn't want there to be any chance that his [future] children would have the same thing. . . . But for the majority of my patients, I don't see genetic tests as necessary: my patients don't ask for them; I don't think they are interested in knowing; there isn't a cure for what they detect. The only thing [these tests] can offer is knowledge. And the only thing they can do is upset their lives. . . . Many of my patients can't even read. They don't know how they'll make it to the end of the week. They don't even have bus fare. They have other problems to resolve besides needing to know whether their condition is genetic.

While less blunt, for the most part the other neighborhood neurologists agreed. Dr Huerta, age 65 and native of South America, stated:

Offering [genetic testing] would depend on the patient's age and my evaluation as to how the patient would benefit from this information. Recently I had a Medicare patient living just above poverty, without relatives and nearly 70 years old. For his symptoms and family history he would have been a good candidate, but with regard to utility, it was zero.

In addition, neighborhood neurologists like Dr Huerta tended to regard genetic testing through a lens of determinism. They said they feared that a genetic diagnosis would communicate the message that one or more of a patient's genes were irreparably damaged and knowing this would lead patients to become more fatalistic about their futures and more passive with regard to their medical care.

Elaborating on this, Dr Huerta added that his own emotions also constrained him from more aggressively pursuing genetic testing for his patients:

I suppose there is always anxiety about [delivering] bad news to patients. This is why I prefer tests that give answers that could be used to work from. An

M.R.I. could show a tumor, which is bad news, but we still may have the option of surgery. With a positive genetic test, there is nothing I can offer and that increases my anxiety. We are trained under the mantra: Intervene, Treat, and Cure, and if I can't [cure] I feel I'm not doing my best.

In sharp contrast with the institution-based and neighborhood neurologists, the specialty clinic neurologists tended to regard genetic testing as of "great value" for the movement disorder patients under their care. Said Dr Weiss, age 40, "It helps patients know what to expect." Dr King voiced a similar perspective:

The ability to give people an answer to the question: What do they have? Are their children at risk? Is there anything that can be done? Without genetic testing, I couldn't answer those questions for many people.

These doctors reflected the view that information, in and of itself, has practical value. Dr Weiss expounded:

There are two [main benefits]. One is that patients, no matter what they have, and no matter how bad or good it is, always feel better if they know what it is. Because one of the things that's frustrating as a physician, and even more frustrating for a patient to hear, is "We don't know." And so you can have a person who has Disease A and a person who has Disease B, and the prognosis and the natural history and the severity of both diseases is identical. But if the person with Disease A knows exactly what it is, can pick up a textbook and read about it or go online and find out something about it, [that person] will do much better and will feel better than the person with Disease B who is, "I don't know what I have. I don't know what's in store for me." And the second is that when you are able to identify the exact disease that somebody has, then you can offer counseling about "Here's the prognosis – so for instance, if you take 100 people with cerebella ataxia, which we now know you have, this is how they do."

Another expressed a similar point of view:

You get a confirmation of diagnosis, which in itself is a relief and enlightening to people, even if in most cases the confirmation does not lead to a different form of treatment. So confirmation, knowing what they have, is beneficial. And if the test is positive, it also opens up the other avenue of discussion of potentially testing other family members, which may be helpful for planning or for knowing what is happening with them.

Some of the specialty clinic neurologists expressed still another value in genetic testing for patients with neurodegenerative disease. They saw in a genetic diagnosis the possibility for navigating new channels of hope. In this regard as well, their views departed from neighborhood neurologists like Dr Huerta who saw genetic testing of little use as a medical tool because it could not help him cure his movement disorder patients and might instead produce feelings of fatalism in patients and their families. In contrast, these specialty clinic neurologists believed that in the absence of meaningful treatment or cure, hope could serve as a substitute for treatment, or even, in and of itself, be of therapeutic value. In this context, the specialty clinic neurologists believed that a genetic diagnosis could offer patients and relatives who had believed they had run out of options a new source of strength and renewed positive outlook that better treatments might someday become available. Dr Singh, a 35-year-old specialty clinic neurologist originally from Asia, elaborated on the perspective that by keeping hope alive, genetic diagnoses could indeed empower patients:

> Saying that we don't know [what you have] closes the door to hope and we have to recognize that hope is nourished in the trust our patients have for us, for our knowledge and our experience. Saying we don't know and showing no willingness to look for answers fuels uncertainty and after a while patients lose hope and they decline.

Dr King was also of the view that "information is power" and believed that by keeping hope alive, information could enhance wellbeing. He explained:

> Frankly, hope is the most important thing we can offer. . . . I know we can't cure our patients and for this reason I think hope is the most important part of any treatment. It makes me more willing to keep the spark of hope burning in a patient or family, as opposed to telling them, "Well, there's nothing that can be done now. There's no cure for this disease. Get your wheelchair now. Don't come back." I think that's one reason that I try to be as good an educator as I can be, because I think the more they understand the better they'll be able to cope with the demands of having to manage chronic progressive neurological disease for which there is no cure at this point.

In sum, while all the neurologists in our study saw abstract value and likely future benefit in the recent dramatic advances in medical genetics, there was far less agreement as to their relevance in their respective medical practices. We saw that the setting in which these clinicians worked proved highly predictive of their views on the subject.

Clinical encounters

We turn now to our observations of 125 clinical encounters to determine the relationship, if any, between views expressed by the neurologists about genetics and their actual interactions with patients and family caregivers when discussing issues surrounding genetics, genetic testing, and genetic diagnoses. Although, as we discussed before, practice setting was significant in the attitudes these clinicians' expressed on the subject, it turned out to be less important for understanding how genetics was discussed in actual clinical consultations.

Given that two-thirds of the neurologists indicated that the vast majority of their movement disorder patients were not, in their view, good candidates for genetic testing, it should come as no surprise to learn that the subject of genetics came up in less than half of the consultations we observed, and that it was most frequently raised in the neurogenetics specialty clinics. When the subject of genetics surfaced in the other two clinical settings, it was frequently introduced by either the patient or relative, not the clinician. Whenever and wherever it was raised, however, for the most part clinicians told patients that genetic diagnoses were at present of little or no utility for curing their disease or arresting the advance of their symptoms. In these types of clinical encounters, discussions about genetics did little to maintain patients' hope.

We saw that the prospect of a genetic diagnosis was not employed in the neighborhood neurology clinics to help patients and family members maintain hope for a variety of reasons, including the clinicians' beliefs that their patients had a limited understanding of the subject, that they lacked the economic resources to pay for genetic testing, and had no interest in genetic issues. We also observed that these physicians felt there was little value in offering such patients genetic testing. Their clinical interactions were consistent with these views. If a patient or family member asked whether there might be a genetic cause for their condition or a test that would help diagnose it, these doctors either sought to discourage the line of questioning, or simply evaded the issue. These dynamics are seen in the following example.

Vicenta Suarez was a 79-year-old monolingual Spanish-speaking woman seeking a diagnosis and treatment for balance problems. She also suffered from hearing loss, anxiety, and depression. Claudia Mendez, her 50-year-old niece and primary caregiver, accompanied her. Vicenta approached Dr Larea and, making direct eye contact, said:

Patient: Doctor, I'm very nervous, very nervous, I don't recognize myself any more. I was a very strong person and now I don't want to do anything, only sleep.

Niece: Doctor, what is making her so nervous? Isn't it something genetic; isn't it like my other aunt [the patient's sister, who was committed to a mental institution]? As the niece, I wish to know.

Doctor: Oh, madam, look, if one is going to look at genetics, everything comes from some deficiency in some gene. What are you going to do? You have to be strong, and try to get better. But genetic, everything is genetic!

In the next example, another neighborhood neurologist, Dr Samora, took a similar approach. The patient, Clarita Ramos, was 87 years old, and, like Vicenta, also a monolingual Spanish speaker. She was accompanied by Eulalia Caicido, her 65-year-old daughter. Their general practitioner referred them for a neurological evaluation because Clarita had recently fallen and was experiencing increasing problems with coordination and hand tremors. Her family doctor had told her that her symptoms could indicate she was suffering from some kind of hereditary ataxia. Here, it is Dr Samora who introduced the subject of genetic testing. Looking at the patient, but speaking to the ethnographer, she volunteered, "With this lady's symptoms, one *could* see what could be found with genetic testing, whether there might be some gene associated with her ataxia symptoms. But honestly, what for?" The conversation continued:

Doctor: If they told me, as your doctor, that it could be genetic, it wouldn't change anything in how I would treat you. If it's for your own interest, at your age, I don't see the benefit. You don't plan to have [more] children [general laughter]. Right, *señora*? If it's for your children and grandchildren, [they are] all grown now, right?

Daughter: Yes, doctor.

Doctor: Well, let's imagine if I decided to order one of those genetic tests. Where would I send you? To [XXX university]? And will they pay attention to you there? We don't know. And you [to the daughter], you told me you have problems with transportation, right?

Daughter: Yes, doctor, we don't have the means to go around in taxis.

Doctor: And that's the other point . . . the means. You're not going to be able to pay for the tests if I send you to a private laboratory, right? And suppose we got lucky and they did the test at [XXX university] and they send me the results and they tell us it's genetic. Then what do we do? I have to send you and your eleven siblings to see if by chance any one of you inherited a gene with the same characteristics? And later, when the results come from their tests, what am I going to do? Send the grand-children [for genetic testing]? And where do I stop? From my perspective the best thing for your mother is to keep her under observation and as comfortable as possible. That's the only thing I feel I should do.

Dr Samora was similarly dismissive during another consultation when Eusábio Rodriguez, who suffered from ataxia and epilepsy, asked whether his problems with epilepsy could have been inherited from his father.

> It is possible to see [if it's genetic]. But to see and know with exactitude, I don't believe it's worth it. In the case of epilepsy, there are tests to determine if dam-aged genes are responsible. But in your case, we don't have your father's test and your father is dead so we'd never know if your father had the same dam-aged genes as yours.

Later in the consultation, apparently partly as a result of explaining why she did not want to pursue a genetic diagnosis, Dr Samora added that she would prescribe the same treatment regimen for this patient regardless of whether or not his epilepsy was genetic in origin.

     We observed other instances during which neighborhood neurologists seemed to regard genetic testing very differently than their patients. Ana Almendra in

Chapter 3 was one example. Ana had been blocked from pursuing genetic testing for H.D. by some of her neurologists because, despite her family history, they doubted that her symptoms were related to the disease. Ultimately, she managed to find one who was willing to order the H.D. test, but he did so on the basis of anxiety and depression, not the physical symptoms she found so disturbing.

These findings are not surprising as the neighborhood neurologists openly admitted limited knowledge of neurogenetics and little experience with genetic testing. We anticipated much more extensive communication about potential and actual genetic issues in the neurogenetics specialty clinics – but this did not necessarily happen. While there were instances of in-depth conversations, we observed many occasions when a genetic test would be characterized simply as an "additional blood test," and others where the clinician's main concern was whether the patient's insurance would cover the costs of genetic testing, not the test results' larger ramifications for patients or family members. In other instances, there appeared to be a radical disconnect between what the patient or family member was seeking and the doctor's response, as is seen in the following example.

Alex Kash was a 27-year-old man who had sought a neurogenetics consultation "for a second opinion about . . . diagnosis and treatment" for the many discolorations, tumors, and moles on his body that other doctors had told him were caused by neurofibromatosis (NF), a genetic disorder of the nervous system with an autosomal dominant inheritance pattern. This means a child has a 50 percent chance of inheriting the disease from an affected parent, although in the case of NF, between 30 to 50 percent of cases occur due to a spontaneous genetic mutation from unknown causes. The patient's mother, Mindy Kash, had accompanied Alex to the consultation. The following conversation took place toward the end of the patient's medical history intake.

Mother: May I ask something? Alex got an NF1 diagnosis. Right?
Doctor: Yes. He has the number one gene causing the problem.
Mother: And it is not hereditary?
Doctor: Right. . . . Because you said that nobody has the same symptoms in your family [referring to Alex's parents].
Mother: But let me tell you a story. My daughter had breast cancer. She had surgery and two years later she got a tumor, benign, in her throat, like her brother, and her doctor, without knowing anything about Alex asked her, "Is there someone in your family with NF?" How could he know?
Doctor: I think it was a very good guess, because your daughter doesn't have your son's symptoms. Another question?

Dr Weiss's terse response to Mindy's question closed off their discussion about a subject of immense interest to her and her children. His seeming impatience on this occasion was surprising: during nearly two years of observations, we found him consistently empathetic, an excellent educator and communicator, and generous with his time. As the consultation continued, Dr Weiss, who had been joined by Dr Barker, passed up other opportunities to provide basic genetic information to the patient and his mother despite being specifically asked. In one instance, Alex asked whether his future children have a "50–50 chance" of inheriting his disease, to which Dr Barker simply said, "Yes." Alex reacted by exclaiming, "That sucks!" But instead of responding to Alex's disappointment with information that might help him better understand his condition in a broader medical context, Dr Barker tried to convince Alex that he should feel lucky that his symptoms were not even worse: "Yes, it does [suck]. But I see many patients that come here for this condition and yours is very, very mild compared with others."

Interaction with specialty clinic neurologists sometimes proved especially disappointing to patients and relatives because of their very high expectations. This was seen in Liz Morgan's case in Chapter 1. Like Liz, most patients seeking neurogenetics consultations had spent years trying to get an accurate diagnosis and had gone to great lengths to secure an appointment at the specialty clinics. They had often waited months and traveled large distances at significant personal cost to see doctors reputed to be the best in their fields. For these patients, the prospect of a genetic diagnosis offered a new, and in many cases what could be considered their last, source of hope. You may remember that Liz's reaction after her initial consultations with Dr King and Dr Dordoni sparked new optimism that a genetic diagnosis might finally set her on the path to improvement. And in fact, she chose to continue to work with them rather than Dr Weiss and Dr Barker because they had restored her feelings of hope. But, as was evidenced in Liz's chapter, although in the short run, patients' and family members' expectations might be met and hope briefly restored, over time they came to the sad realization that like all the other doctors they had consulted, the specialty clinic neurologists had no magic bullets, and hope gave way to even deeper disappointment.

It is important to add that not every clinical interaction involving genetics or genetic issues was problematic. We also observed situations in which patients or family members were given accurate information and sensitive straightforward answers to their questions. For instance, we observed an encounter between the institution-based general neurologist Dr Green and Agatha Brook, a 57-year-old woman unexpectedly diagnosed with Huntington's disease the previous year, Brian, Agatha's husband, and Courtney, the couple's 30-year-old daughter. The purpose of the consultation was to confirm Agatha's H.D. diagnosis and to determine whether there might be better treatments, in particular for falling and incontinence, which Courtney said she thought might be caused by her mother's medication. In the course of Agatha's clinical assessment, Brian volunteered:

Husband: Dr Cross [our family doctor] was surprised about the test result. He thought it could be dementia.

Doctor: Huntington's *is* an uncommon disease. A general neurologist would see maybe one case a year. When there is no family history, it can be difficult to diagnose . . . [But in our movement disorders clinic we're more familiar with this disease and] when we see that the age is right, even if there is no family history of chorea, we may think about Huntington's disease because in some cases a parent died before showing symptoms or sometimes a parent is not the parent the patient thinks. I don't suggest this is the case for you.

After the assessment was over and they were discussing Agatha's medication, Dr Green came back to the subject of genetics, "We haven't talked about the genetics [of H.D.]. I assume you know that if one person has the disease, her children and siblings have a 50 percent chance of carrying the gene . . . ." He offered a bit more detail about how the disease typically affects patients over time and told them a little about the history of the gene's discovery. When Brian expressed his fear that his wife's condition would advance quickly, Dr Green replied that the rate of progression is variable and depends on the individual. Courtney then asked:

Daughter: Is the blood test [for H.D.] accurate?
Doctor: Very accurate.
Husband: How accurate?
Daughter: Is it 99 percent accurate?
Doctor: Yes, 99 percent.

Possibly anticipating her unvoiced concerns, Dr Green continued:

There is the issue of pre-symptomatic testing for you. It's a very difficult decision. There are some people who carry the gene but they don't have symptoms until very late in life. If they get tested they have the burden of the knowledge most of their life and fear of the disease even if they don't show any symptoms until very late in their life. I had a young patient with Huntington's. Both his parents were still living and he said that he didn't have any family history. But I asked him to bring his parents at the next consultation so we could further examine the issue with them. The mother got very angry that we had discussed the issue. The father obviously had early symptoms. But she didn't want to know in advance when he was going to develop the [full-blown] disease.

In this consultation, Dr Green appeared very sensitive to the family's concerns. He provided clear and simple but also accurate explanations in language the husband and daughter could understand, and used real life examples from his own clinical experiences to help orient them to some of the larger relevant issues. Although we anticipated we would find similar depth in discussions of genetics and genetic issues in other clinical settings, as the examples above have shown, this seldom occurred.

Discussion

In this chapter we described some of the challenges consequent to the introduction of genetics into mainstream medical care. Dr Huerta got to the core of the paradoxes when he said, "We are trained under the mantra: 'Intervene, Treat, and Cure,' and if I can't [cure] I feel I'm not doing my best." Yet any neurologist who works with movement disorder patients knows this "mantra" will always be simply an ideal:

most of the diseases they are called upon to treat can neither be prevented nor cured, and few interventions can do much, if anything, to slow their inevitable course. Partly in response to what might appear to be a highly demoralizing situation, some clinicians sought to turn hope into a therapeutic intervention. In this regard, Cheryl Mattingly has brilliantly shown in her exegesis on the distinct cultural meanings associated with hope in American medical care:

> Hope itself is best understood as an active cultural practice . . . that [paradoxically] lives side by side with despair. . . . Hope most centrally involves the practice of creating, or trying to create, lives worth living even in the midst of suffering, even with no cure in sight. This is why I have chosen to speak of hope as a *practice*, rather than simply an emotion or a cultural attitude.
>
> (Mattingly n.d.: Chapter 1, pp. 5, 11; see also Good *et al.* 1990)

Given this reality, what *are* the benefits that a genetic diagnosis can offer, and to whom? The narratives of many doctors, particularly the neighborhood M.D.s, revealed that while they valued the potential benefits from advances in genetic knowledge, they saw no practical use for them with their patients. In this, they reflected the widespread view that the only justification for genetic testing is to obtain information that can be acted upon (Dreifus 2008). While never articulated directly, these neighborhood neurologists' attitudes may also have reflected their own insecurities associated with discussing genetic issues with patients and relatives, given their radically limited knowledge of the subject. But perhaps paradoxically, while these doctors saw little value in information for its own sake in their clinical practices, they told us that should they themselves experience movement disorder symptoms, they might well pursue genetic testing for diagnostic and planning purposes.

However, many patients in our study, along with a number of the institution-based and specialty clinic neurologists, disagreed with the view that knowledge that cannot be acted upon has no value. Dr Weiss, for instance, while not a strong advocate for genetic testing, said that having *any* diagnosis, whether or not it would lead to better treatment or alter the course of a disease, helped both doctors and patients. He said patients with a diagnosis "do much better and . . . feel better" than those with exactly the same symptoms who have none. He also recounted his frustration when he was forced to tell a patient, "We [just] don't know [what you have]." In his opinion, any diagnosis, no matter how grave and even without immediate clinical significance, can keep hope alive.

Dr Weiss's views on the subject raise a number of provocative questions: Do neurodegenerative (or other) patients with a diagnosis actually "feel better" and perhaps, in some sense, "do better" than those without one? Do patients with a diagnosis feel more hopeful because they have a framework for understanding their experiences? Do patients who feel hopeful have better outcomes? And in this regard, is hope an absolute or relative condition? A related question is whether knowledge necessarily leads to "empowerment." Dr Green was among those who believed that a genetic diagnosis could facilitate planning for patients and at-risk family members. This view contrasted with those of the neighborhood neurologists, who believed that possessing knowledge that could not be acted upon produced fatalism and passivity.

None of the clinicians who believed that genetic testing could, indeed, provide clear benefits for patients regarded the larger ramifications of offering these tests to healthy family members as necessarily positive. Marcia Van Riper illustrates some of the issues in her research with healthy women at very high risk for genetic forms of breast and ovarian cancer. She offers compelling narrative accounts that detail why some chose not to be tested so they would not have to live with the burden of knowledge that they had inherited one of the known breast cancer genes (Van Riper 2005).

Whether most patients with a neurodegenerative disease would want or welcome a genetic diagnosis is a separate question. This was indeed the case for those in our study, who we met because they were seeking a diagnosis, a second opinion, and/or better treatment for their symptoms. Most, if not all, shared Dr Weiss's perspective that any diagnosis, no matter how grave, was preferable to not having one at all. Gerry Reedson, for instance, another of our study participants, who had been diagnosed with Huntington's just before we met, starkly brought home this insight when he recounted his sense of relief upon learning his diagnosis. Given his family history, he had suspected that some of his symptoms were due to H.D., but feared Huntington's might not be his only problem. Amazingly to us, when Gerry learned that it was "just" Huntington's from which he was suffering, he felt an enormous burden had been lifted!

At the same time, we do not know whether patients who opted out of the medical system or otherwise gave up on discovering the cause of their symptoms might have become more motivated to seek genetic testing if they were exposed to better education on the subject or perhaps had health insurance that covered its costs. We also do not know whether reducing uncertainty through an accurate diagnosis would lead hope to collapse as the neighborhood doctors predicted or, as the specialists asserted, that a genetic diagnosis would motivate neurodegenerative patients to become more involved in their medical care and feel greater control over their lives. In fact, the scientific literature lends support to both views: while some studies of patients suffering from number of diverse conditions find that they may react fatalistically to the knowledge that their disease is genetic, other research has shown that many such patients do not necessarily regard their disease as immutable but think that only a biologically based treatment (i.e. a drug but not a behavioral intervention such as a low fat diet) can have an effect (Marteau and Weinman 2006). That said, from our own data it should be clear that these clinicians' beliefs, attitudes, and values about the practicality of genetic testing – as much as any specific scientific understandings or technical knowledge – proved to be driving forces in their decisions about whether and when to offer the tests.

In this chapter, we examined the views of neurologists who worked in different types of practice settings about the benefits and challenges genetic testing brought to their clinical practices. We also looked at some of these clinicians' interactions with patients and family members, and saw some of the complex issues that arise as a consequence of the proliferation of genetic testing for the diagnosis of a group of neurological disorders that have no effective treatment or cure. Yet we are only just beginning to understand the full extent of the impact of genetics and genomics on health and disease. As our knowledge increases, many more patients and doctors will be having conversations on these subjects and will be increasingly faced with the kinds of dilemmas we have described. This brief exploration of the views of our small sample of neurologists is, we hope, a first step toward charting a more constructive direction for those discussions.

Final reflections

We set out to examine the impact of recent developments in medical genetics and genetic testing on the management of neurodegenerative diseases. Until now, neither large-scale surveys nor in-depth analyses have investigated the significance of such advances for neurologists, their patients, or patients' family members. The so-called Hippocratic injunction to "above all, do no harm" has guided treatment and cure in Western medicine for thousands of years. But new understandings about the role of heredity in many common disorders including neurological ones and the development of genetic tests for diagnosing them are challenging the continued relevance and application of Hippocratic values for today's medicine, given the limitations of treatments and lack of cures for virtually all of the conditions that can be detected through genetic testing.

Despite the fanfare with which the media heralds each new advance in genetic medicine, we found that most patients, family caregivers, and clinicians in our study knew little, if anything, about the existence of genetic testing for neurodegenerative disorders. Moreover, while many patients who received genetic diagnoses were relieved to have added scientific certainty about what they were suffering from, that type of diagnosis, in and of itself, did not alleviate the patients' suffering nor the terms under which they would live out the remainder of their disrupted lives. Indeed, except for patients diagnosed with the very well known disorder of Huntington's disease, we saw no evidence among either patients or their relatives of the formation of either new social groups or novel identity practices that might derive from a newfound biosocial identity based on a positive genetic test.

Much more consequential for both patients and family caregivers was the everyday burden of living with neurodegenerative diseases. Patients found most devastating their progressive loss of independence and the erosion of their core identity; family caregivers' greatest concerns were the perpetual emotional trauma of caring for a loved one with a progressively disabling disease, along with the fear that they too might someday find themselves in the same position.

During the three years we spent interacting with patients and their families, we were continually anguished by the "dark prophecies" their narratives foretold. Nevertheless, as we strove to comprehend the depth of their experiences, we were surprised and heartened to perceive intermittent rays of hope and optimism. We saw that even in the face of a devastating diagnosis, or when confronting the disappointment that yet another new treatment had failed and symptoms were continuing to grow more severe, patients and family caregivers somehow managed to bounce back, readjust, and forge new strategies to keep life moving and hope alive.

We found that despite relentless, incremental increases in impairment, most patients sought any means they could manage to remain engaged in helping to reshape the downshifting contours of their daily lives. Some worked to create new living situations more conducive to their present and projected capabilities. Others reconfigured family relations; still others focused on staying informed about new medical advances that might, some day, conceivably, cure their symptoms or at least ameliorate their otherwise inexorable course.

Part I introduced Liz Morgan and Ana Almendra to illustrate the processes by which patients with neurodegenerative symptoms that defy diagnosis may continue to search for answers in worlds filled with shadows. Their stories revealed the lengths to which patients may have to go to discover the root causes of their symptoms, the demoralizing effects of receiving contradictory medical information (from which it could be extremely difficult to extract meaning), and their experiences with genetic testing, which in the end, fell short of their expectations that it would offer a meaningful solution to their medical problems or provide clarity as to their current circumstances.

Liz's inconclusive genetic test, which she had seen as her "last hope" for an accurate diagnosis, shattered her trust in biomedicine, punctured her hopes for recovery, and seriously jeopardized her willingness to continue her life increasingly marked by suffering. Eventually, however, the promise of alternative medicine appeared upon the horizon to inspire Liz and her husband to keep going.

Ana also faced serious obstacles in the course of her quest for an accurate diagnosis and treatment. But being younger and less impaired, Ana was able to muster the determination to go on with her life with a greater sense of purpose than Liz. Ultimately, Ana's decision to proceed with genetic testing created a different type of dilemma: despite her positive test result, doctors refused to agree that her painful "sensations" were early H.D. symptoms. Still Ana refused to be defeated: she continued to search for medical answers in the hope that some new doctor could better explain the cause of her symptoms or point the way to a new drug that might offer a cure or slow the inexorable progression of her disease. It was mainly the need to provide for her two young children that motivated Ana to remain asymptomatic for as long as possible. Yet paradoxically those very children who gave Ana her reason for living might never have been born had she received her H.D. diagnosis years earlier, when she first sought it. Ana's narrative, then, further revealed some of the complexities of offering genetic testing for conditions that can be neither prevented, cured, nor meaningfully treated, but which could dramatically change the course of a patient's life.

In Part II we offered Enrique Silvestre's and Carlos Estrada's stories to exemplify ways in which patients who receive devastating diagnoses may reinvent their lives as they try to come to terms with growing infirmity. These men, along with others we met in the course of this investigation, appeared nothing less than heroic in their daily struggles to preserve their identities and live their lives in the face of increasingly compromised functioning. In Enrique's case, although this meant giving up the proud self-image of a man literally living the "American Dream," he nonetheless managed to sustain his even more valued identity of a man still in control of his destiny. Carlos's efforts also revolved around maintaining a sense of power by preserving his identity as head of his household, even as he was forced to relinquish his role as the family's chief breadwinner. For both men, their illnesses provided incentives, albeit unwelcome ones, to forge ahead and reconfigure new lives.

One of our chief objectives had been to understand what, if anything, might be uniquely meaningful about a genetic diagnosis for already-ill patients. In this regard, our study differs in a major way from most other research on the subject, which has looked mainly at genetic testing decisions made by healthy, asymptomatic individuals deemed to be "at risk" for a variety of disorders with a known genetic cause or contributory factor. This means that even if they should decide to be tested and they test positive, they might still never develop the condition, so the test results may never have any concrete impact on their lives. We, on the other hand, worked exclusively with people who were *already* very ill and desperately searching for the cause of their symptoms. In their situations, a diagnosis, genetic or otherwise, might not offer the possibility of prevention, cure, or even treatments to slow the course of their disease. However, such a diagnosis could provide a framework or set of parameters for understanding and, in some cases, removing the stigma of their undiagnosed, and therefore doubly troubling, illness experiences.

In our journey to understand the significance of genetic information in the lives of neurodegenerative patients, we took a relevant detour from our main focus on patients to learn how such information was communicated, conceptualized, and used by family caregivers and clinicians. Part III focused on these issues. We showed that family caregivers, through their approach to care (for example, encouraging or discouraging autonomy, or caregivers' degree of interest in genetic and other types of medical information), could significantly affect patients' sense of wellbeing and their willingness to continue treatment. We further found that caregivers could – or could seek to – play central roles in patients' decisions about genetic testing, much as they did in other aspects of their relatives' lives. But from patients' perspectives, much more important than the assistance they received from family caregivers with daily activities and medical decisions was whether they helped to keep hope alive by sustaining continuity, independence, and valued identities.

When we began this investigation, genetic tests for movement disorder symptoms were just being introduced, and we wanted to assess their relevance not just for patients and families but also for clinicians. Because genetic testing is relevant for only a sub-sample of movement disorder patients, we did not necessarily expect to find much discussion on the subject in the offices of the general neurologists with whom we worked. Our clinicians' chapter showed, however, that even in the neurogenetics specialty clinics we worked in, there was far less discussion of genetics than we had anticipated, and further, that outside those specialty clinics, such conversations were often initiated by patients or family members, not clinicians.

We also discovered a vast gap between the understandings of patients and family caregivers on the one hand, and clinicians on the other, with regard to the meaning and relevance of a genetic diagnosis for patients with neurodegenerative disease. Many patients and family caregivers assumed it would help with actual disease management, while most neurologists considered the main utilities to be extra-medical, such as for reproductive planning or helping patients qualify for medical benefits and other types of assistance (e.g. a new residence, a home health aide).

We also saw how and why the specific type of practice setting in which clinicians worked was critical in constraining or promoting offers of genetic testing. Several factors contributed to this pattern, but of particular importance was the fact that the neighborhood neurologists in our investigation saw mainly low-income Spanish-speaking immigrants with little formal education, who the clinicians regarded as unsuitable candidates for genetic testing. This was true for a number of reasons. One was the presumption that such patients would be unable to understand "sophisticated" genetic information; another was the belief that they would be unwilling and/or unable to devote scarce economic resources to tests of this sort. These neighborhood neurologists' views differed markedly from the specialty clinic physicians, who generally treated a more affluent and more educated patient population. These doctors tended to feel that, in and of itself, information had value, whether or not it had actual clinical relevance. In contrast, the more pragmatic neighborhood neurologists saw genetic tests for their patients as useful only if they provided information that could be acted upon.

The experiences of Enrique Silvestre and Carlos Estrada illuminated these dynamics, while offering interesting points of convergence and divergence. Although both men were Spanish-speaking immigrants with limited formal education, Enrique was from an affluent family and since coming to the U.S. had experienced far more economic success than Carlos (perhaps not coincidently). Also, while Carlos's movement disorder symptoms began when he was still a young child, Enrique's emerged only in adulthood. You will recall that Dr Larea, one of the neighborhood neurologists, had cared for both men. As we saw in Chapter 7, Dr Larea regarded genetic testing as having very limited relevance for his patients. However he did refer both men for testing. Enrique, in fact, had sought a neurological consultation specifically to have a genetic test. He wanted to confirm his previous clinical diagnosis so he could then "rationally" engage in work and family-related planning. He also had the means to pay for testing. Dr Larea was willing to comply because he could see its value and because payment posed no obstacle.

Carlos's experience was entirely different. In his case, it was Dr Larea who had suggested genetic testing based on his symptoms and his medical and family histories, despite the fact that Carlos lacked the means to pay for the test. Dr Larea was willing to undergo considerable inconvenience to help his patient get tested because he knew that otherwise Carlos would have great difficulty qualifying for much-needed long-term disability benefits to which he was entitled. Dr Larea perceived explicit reasons for having both Enrique and Carlos tested, although in neither case would the result enable Dr Larea to offer them more effective or meaningful medical care.

Deeply probing the complex realities of living with neurodegenerative disease and the potential and actual meanings of a genetic diagnosis for patients, family caregivers, and clinicians, we came to see that some of the preconceptions we held at the outset of our research were, to varying degrees, off the mark.

For one thing, we had anticipated that the specificity of a genetic diagnosis would be a welcome antidote to the uncertainty patients and family caregivers had endured during their protracted quests for a determinative diagnosis. This view, while valid, was much too simple. The experiences of a number of study participants, Ana Almendra and Carlos Estrada among them, taught us that given the current state of medical knowledge, while a genetic diagnosis can provide general information about likely patterns of a disease trajectory, it barely scratches the surface in offering precise medical information about what individuals with that diagnosis can expect. Prognoses remained clouded and doubt continued to darken patients' perspectives on their life situations.

Still, no matter how grave the diagnosis, it was also generally met with immense, albeit not necessarily un-ambivalent feelings of relief. We saw this in Chapter 6 in the unburdening Gerry Reedson felt on receiving his Huntington's diagnosis. Enrique Silvestre reported something similar when he explained that he had pursued genetic testing to confirm his clinical diagnosis so he could "grab the bull by the horns before it got [him first]." So what many might imagine would be the worst medical news possible, was experienced as empowering by patients like Gerry and Enrique, demonstrating that *any* firm diagnosis, however grave, can help reduce medical uncertainty, regardless of the technology employed.

Second, in studying genetic conditions, we had anticipated that fears of stigma often associated with inherited disorders might influence patients' and family caregivers' willingness to pursue genetic testing. This assumption also proved too narrow. We mainly saw that patients like Ana Almendra and, eventually, Ana's own mother, were eager to pursue genetic testing, even in cases when doctors thought it was inappropriate for them. In part, as mentioned, this had to do with the reduction of uncertainty that any diagnosis brings. But many study participants like Ana, and Maria Estrada in Chapter 4, also hoped that a genetic diagnosis would confer legitimacy, a prospect far more important to them than any fears of possible stigma.

We had similarly imagined that family members might also be fearful about potential stigma should their afflicted relative receive a genetic diagnosis. This, too, was not necessarily the case. Family members like Mary Solomon in Chapter 5 found the benefits of an accurate diagnosis for their relatives' symptoms far more meaningful than any potential stigma; others such as Carlos's mother, Eduarda, reported that the diagnosis made her son's experiences more understandable and thereby easier to endure.

Still, as we saw in various chapters, feelings of stigma were not entirely absent from patients with neurodegenerative disease. It was something they lived with and talked about, and that we regularly observed. Those who had been symptomatic but undiagnosed since adolescence or childhood had already endured years of being falsely labeled as lazy, crazy, malingering, or alcoholic, and sometimes all of these. This was poignantly illustrated in the Estrada family's narratives where

Maria fervently wished that her and her siblings' symptoms be recognized as *real*; similarly, as a child, Ana Almendra had experienced distress and confusion when relatives compared her with her alcoholic father, who she remembered mainly as short-tempered, rude, and aggressive. For patients like these, the legitimacy of a diagnosis, genetic or otherwise, was cathartic and deeply validating.

Third, like some of the neighborhood neurologists in this investigation, we had expected patients and family caregivers to react with a sense of fatalism to a genetic diagnosis. Instead, as narratives like Mary Solomon's and Roland Pilgrim's revealed, we found that a genetic diagnosis could also bring hope. We had also believed that integral to lay views about genetics were notions of determinism and immutability. But patients' and family caregivers' concepts of genetics were not necessarily deterministic, and in fact, proved surprisingly complex.

Many patients and family caregivers, however, erroneously regarded a genetic diagnosis, like any other, as a step toward prevention or cure. They held strong beliefs in the value of information, whether or not it could be acted upon immediately. And perhaps because many Americans want to see themselves as the masters of their own destiny, study participants like Liz Morgan were deeply convinced of the efficacy of self-help activities, especially the acquisition of new information, dietary modifications, and positive thinking, seeing them, along with faith and hope, as possessing actual therapeutic power. Some clinicians, who similarly regarded "hope" as therapeutic, especially for those suffering conditions for which there is no possibility of cure, reinforced this perspective. But sadly, as we also often saw, and was exemplified by Liz's story, without tangible results, the therapeutic psychological benefits of hope can quickly crumble, spiraling patients toward even greater uncertainty and darker despair. In situations like these, family caregivers, like Liz's husband Paul, usually came to the patient's rescue.

Genetic tests are increasingly being marketed directly to the public, accompanied by extravagant claims that simple genetic mechanisms may be at the core of many physiological, psychological, and emotional processes, and ostensibly complex behaviors; there are no signs that these practices will abate anytime soon. Whereas in 1997 there were 332 labs and biotech companies engaged in the development or clinical use of genetic tests, by 2009 there were 603 labs testing for 1,715 different genetic diseases. Further advances in gene discovery techniques such as genome-wide association studies will undoubtedly continue this trend, and the currently $2 billion dollar genetic testing industry is projected to grow to $15 billion over the next ten years. But anecdotal reports indicate that these costly genetic tests are often inappropriately ordered by physicians or incorrectly interpreted by them. This situation can only grow worse.

Accelerated marketing efforts designed to generate excitement in those who want to glimpse backward into their genetic heritage or forward, to learn the extent of their vulnerability to particular diseases, have also raised serious concerns among bioethicists and other social analysts for numerous reasons, including the fact that the information genetic tests produce is difficult for physicians to interpret, let alone for the general public. In addition, misinterpretation of test findings can lead to incorrect or unnecessary medical treatments or other interventions. Worse still, given our present limited understanding of the role of genetic factors in most disease processes, genetic test results can produce a false sense of reassurance – or baseless, unwarranted anxiety; moreover, as we saw, they can add new types of stress to family relationships or exacerbate existing ones.

Widespread marketing of genetic testing raises additional issues for people who are already ill and for the clinicians who treat them. Increasingly, gravely ill patients like those we met in the course of this investigation and family members who help care for them are curious about the relevance of genetic testing for their own situations. Many come to their doctors with false hopes as to what the tests can do for them. But most clinicians, like the majority of the neurologists in this investigation, have little personal experience with genetic testing, are not particularly well trained or informed in the subject, and, understandably, do not feel very comfortable discussing it. And as more and more tests come to market, the problem is growing more acute. Physicians will become increasingly less able to accurately answer patients' and relatives' questions about genetic tests and to anticipate their concerns about genetic issues during routine office consultations.

Elsewhere, researchers have explicated other factors that can impede meaningful discussion between patients and doctors about genetic testing. Communication on the subject is generally complex, not just because the basic concepts of genetics may be difficult for lay people to understand, but because information derived from genetic testing has the potential to materially alter one's sense of self, family relationships, and actual and anticipated life programs and plans. Moreover, established techniques for conveying genetic information run counter to the conventions of clinical medicine, which proceed from the assumption that patients consult with doctors to avail their medical expertise. In genetic medicine, clinicians are expected to offer information and answer questions, but to avoid direct recommendations about a course of action.

More mundane obstacles that also constrain meaningful communication about genetic testing in standard medical consultations include time pressures, insufficient compensation for patient counseling, structural impediments to getting referrals to specialists approved in a simple and timely manner, and serving patients whose needs may be far greater than clinicians can realistically meet in the course of their busy practices.

These are largely interconnected and vexing problems for which there are no simple solutions. There is, however, one obvious, at least short-term remedy. Clinicians can become much more proactive in referring patients and relatives seeking information about genetic testing to certified genetic counselors. This happened all too seldom during our research. In addition to expertise in the science of medical genetics, professional counselors are specially trained to provide clear, simple, and accurate information in language lay people can understand. Further, they are qualified to constructively explore with patients and family members the ethical, emotional, and psychological issues that genetic testing can provoke. In fact, the immediate need for certified genetic counselors throughout the globe far exceeds their actual numbers, and the demand for their services will continue to grow exponentially as genetic testing becomes more ubiquitous in routine medical care and genetic issues gain even greater centrality.

Over the longer term, it would certainly be possible to create a much better environment for clinical communication about genetic testing and the larger issues it can raise. In addition to continuing to work more closely with genetic counselors, physicians could themselves receive more training in genetics, genetic testing, and relevant bioethics. Office visits could allow sufficient time for talking about what genetic testing does and does not offer for a particular patient's care. Given the intricacies of the topic, to communicate most effectively, clinicians could employ real life examples drawn from their own clinical experience. Clinical protocols could be modified to cover issues associated with informed consent, privacy, stigma, and discrimination. These topics are extremely important given the potential likelihood for a patient's genetic testing decisions and results to have significant ramifications for the larger family group. To optimize the benefits of genetic testing, clinicians need to consider not simply the importance of the tests' clinically relevant information, but the patient's associated psychological and emotional needs. Every effort should be expended to help ensure that patients have the necessary tools to understand the medical, emotional, economic, and family implications of their test results.

Our research was inspired and guided by the dedicated efforts of family caregivers and physicians. But it was the amazing courage of patients living each day with progressively devastating neurodegenerative diseases and their unflinching struggle to persevere that invigorated and propelled our work the most. While genetic testing is just starting to make inroads into neurology clinical practices, it is sure to play an increasingly important role in the years ahead. As this comes to pass, we hope the patients', family caregivers' and clinicians' stories, viewpoints, and experiences offered here, along with our interpretations of them, will help pave the way to make this transformation more enlightened, constructive, and useful for those confronted with the kinds of situations we have documented here.

Notes

Introduction

1 Genetics is the scientific study of heredity; genomics is the study of interactions among genes and between genes and environmental factors.

2 The terms "movement disorder symptoms" and "neurodegenerative symptoms" are used interchangeably throughout this text to refer to the symptoms patients in this study were experiencing as a consequence of neurodegenerative disease processes. Although many of the disorders we studied often involved cognitive impairment, the patients who participated in our research were not significantly cognitively impaired.

3 All study procedures were approved by the relevant institutional review board (IRB) of our home institution, as well as the IRBs of other institutional field sites. Signed consent forms were obtained from all study participants.

Introduction to Part I

1 All proper names are pseudonyms.

1 A new door opening

1 A clinical diagnosis is a working hypothesis based on a physician's interpretations of a patient's clinical signs and presenting symptoms.

2 Destination unknown

1 "The genetic defect responsible for HD is a small sequence of DNA on chromosome 4 in which several base pairs are repeated many, many times. The normal gene has three DNA bases, composed of the sequence CAG. In people with HD, the sequence abnormally repeats itself dozens of times. Over time – and with each successive generation – the number of CAG repeats may expand further. Individuals who do not have HD usually have 28 or fewer CAG repeats. Individuals with HD usually have 40 or more repeats . . . The largest number of CAG repeats of anyone studied so far [is] nearly 100." Huntington's Disease Information Page, NIH National Institute of Neurological Disorders and Stroke, 2008, http://www.ninds.nih.gov.

5 Maintaining hope and independence in the face of despair

1 Many patients in our study did not have family caregivers sufficiently involved in their lives (or in their care) for it to have been meaningful for us to interview them. For

this reason the size of the family caregiver sample is much smaller than the patient sample.

6 The neurologists' conundrum

1 Clinicians whose birthplace is not indicated were from the U.S.

Bibliography

Ablon, J. (1995) '"The elephant man" as "self" and "other": the psychosocial costs of a misdiagnosis', *Social Science and Medicine*, 40: 1481–90.

Alper, J.S., Ard, C., Asch, A., Beckwith, J., Conrad, P. and Geller, L.N. (eds) (2002) *The Double-Edged Helix: Social Implications of Genetics in a Diverse Society*, Baltimore: Johns Hopkins University Press.

Aminoff, M.J., Greenberg, R.R. and Simon, D. (2005) *Clinical Neurology*, 6th edn, New York: McGraw-Hill Medical.

Anonymous (1996) 'Living with the threat of Huntington's disease', in T. Marteau and M. Richards (eds) *The Troubled Helix: Social and Psychological Implications of the New Human Genetics*, Cambridge: Cambridge University Press.

Armstrong, D., Michie, S. and Marteau, T. (1998) 'Revealed identity: a study of the process of genetic counseling', *Social Science and Medicine*, 47: 1653–58.

Atkinson, P., Parsons, E. and Featherstone, K. (2001) 'Professional constructions of family and kinship in medical genetics', *New Genetics and Society*, 20: 5–24.

Becker, G. (1980) *Growing Old in Silence*, Berkeley: University of California Press.

—— (1997) *Disrupted Lives: How People Create Meaning in a Chaotic World*, Berkeley: University of California Press.

—— (2000) *The Elusive Embryo: How Women and Men Approach New Reproductive Technologies*, Berkeley: University of California Press.

Beckham, K. and Giordano, J.A. (1986) 'Illness and impairment in elderly couples: implications for marital therapy', *Family Relations*, 35: 257–64.

Bertram, L., Blacker, D., Mullin, K., Keeney, D., Jones, J., Basu, S., Yhu, S., McInnis, M.G., Go, R.C., Vekrellis, K., Selkoe, D.J., Saunders A.J. and Tanzi, R.E. (2000) 'Evidence for genetic linkage of Alzheimer's disease to chromosome 10q', *Science*, 290: 2302–03.

Bharadwaj, A. (2002) 'Uncertain risk: genetic screening for susceptibility to haemochromatosis', *Health, Risk, and Society*, 4: 227–40.

Bharadwaj, A., Atkinson, P. and Clarke, A. (2006) 'Medical classification and the experience of genetic haemochromatosis', in P. Atkinson, H. Greenslade and P. Glasner (eds) *New Genetics, New Identities*, London: Routledge.

Bird, T.D. (1999) 'Risks and benefits of DNA testing for neurogenetic disorders', *Seminars in Neurology*, 58: 253–59.

Bird, T.D. and Bennett, R.L. (1995) 'Why do DNA testing? Practical and ethical implications of new neurogenetic tests', *Annals of Neurology*, 38: 141–46.

Blasko, J. (2006) 'Genomics and neurology: a medical view', *Health Progress*, 87: 62–67.

Bohnam, V. and Terry, S. (2008) 'A vision for the future of genomics: education and community engagement: a white paper for the national human genome research institute'.

Online. Available HTTP: http://www.genome.gov/pfv.cfm?pageID=27529214 (accessed 15 May 2009).

Boorse, C. (2004) 'On the distinction between illness and disease', in A.L. Caplan, J.C. McCartney and D.A. Sisti (eds) *Health, Disease, and Illness: Concepts in Medicine*, Washington, DC: Georgetown University Press.

Bowker, G.C. and Starr, S.L. (1999) *Sorting Things Out: Classification and Its Consequence*, Cambridge: The MIT Press.

Broadstock, M., Michie, S. and Marteau, T. (2000) 'Psychological consequences of predictive genetic testing: a systematic review', *European Journal of Human Genetics*, 8: 731–38.

Browner, C.H. and Preloran, H.M. (2000a) 'Latinas, amniocentesis and the discourse of choice', *Culture, Medicine, and Psychiatry*, 24: 353–75.

—— (2000b) 'Interpreting low-income Latinas' amniocentesis refusals', *Hispanic Journal of Behavioral Sciences*, 22: 346–68.

Browner, C.H. and Press, N. (1995) 'The normalization of prenatal diagnostic screening', in F. Ginsburg and R. Rapp (eds) *Conceiving the New World Order: The Global Politics of Reproduction*, Berkeley: University of California Press.

Browner, C.H., Preloran, H.M. and Cox, S.J. (1999) 'Ethnicity, bioethics, and prenatal diagnosis: the amniocentesis decisions of Mexican-origin women and their partners', *American Journal of Public Health*, 89: 1658–66.

Burgess, M.M. and D'agincourt-Canning, L. (2001) 'Genetic testing for hereditary disease: attending to relational responsibility', *Journal of Clinical Ethics*, 12: 361–72.

Burgess, M.M., Laberge, C.M. and Knoppers, B.M. (1998) 'Bioethics for clinicians: ethics and genetics in medicine', *Canadian Medical Association Journal*, 158: 1309–13.

Burke, P.J. and Reitzes, D.C. (1981) 'The link between identity and role performance', *Social Psychology Quarterly*, 44: 83–92.

Burke, W. and Emery, J. (2002) 'Genetics education for primary-care provider', *Nature Reviews: Genetics*, 3: 561–66.

Burke, W., Pinsky, L.E. and Press, N.A. (2001) 'Categorizing genetic tests to identify their ethical, legal, and social implications', *American Journal of Medical Genetics*, 106: 233–40.

Burke, W., Acheson, L., Bodkin, J., Bridges, K., Davis, A., Evans, J., Frias, J., Hanson, J., Kahn, N., Kahn, R., Lanier, D., Pinsky, L.E., Press, N., Lloyd-Puryear, M.A., Rich, E., Stevens, N., Thomson, E., Wartman, S. and Wilson, M. (2002) 'Genetics in primary care: a USA faculty development initiative', *Community Genetics*, 5: 138–46.

Bury, M. (1982) 'Chronic illness as biographic disruption', *Sociology of Health and Illness*, 4: 167–82.

Callanan, N.P. and LeRoy, B.S. (2006) 'Genetic counseling approach to genetic testing', in N.F. Sharpe and R.F. Carter (eds) *Genetic Testing: Care, Consent, and Liability*, Hoboken, NJ: John Wiley & Sons, Inc.

Capps, L. and Ochs, E. (1995) *Constructing Panic: The Discourse of Agoraphobia*, Cambridge, MA: Harvard University Press.

Cebik, L.B. (1984) *Fictional Narrative and Truth: An Epistemic Analysis*, Lanham: University Press of America.

Chapple, A., May, C. and Campion, P. (1995) 'Lay understanding of genetic disease: a British study of families attending a genetic counseling service', *Journal of Genetic Counseling*, 4: 247–53.

Chavez, L.R., Hubbell, F.A., McMullin, J.M., Martinez, R.G. and Mishra, S.I. (1995) 'Structure and meaning in models of breast and cervical cancer risk factors: a comparison of perceptions among Latinas, Anglo women, and physicians', *Medical Anthropology Quarterly*, 9: 40–74.

Conrad, P. and Gabe, J. (eds) (2000) *Sociological Perspectives on the New Genetics*, Oxford: Blackwell Publishers.

Cox, S.M. and McKellin, W. (1999) '"There's this thing in our family": predictive testing and the construction of risk for Huntington disease', *Sociology of Health and Illness*, 21: 622–46.

Cunningham-Burley, S. (2008) 'Public and professional understandings of genetics', in *Encyclopedia of Life Sciences*, Chichester: John Wiley & Sons, Ltd. Online. Available HTTP: http://mrw.interscience.wiley.com/emrw/9780470015902/els/article/a0005865 (accessed 15 May 2009).

Cunningham-Burley, S. and Boulton, M. (2000) 'The social context of the new genetics', in G.L. Albrecht, R. Fitzpatrick and S.C. Scrimshaw (eds) *Handbook of Social Studies in Health and Medicine*, London: Sage.

D'agincourt-Canning, L. (2001) 'Experiences of genetic risk: disclosure and the gendering of responsibility,' *Bioethics*, 15: 231–47.

D'Andrade, R. (1991) 'The identification of schemas in naturalistic data', in M.J. Horowitz (ed.) *Person Schemas and Maladaptive Interpersonal Patterns*, Chicago: University of Chicago Press.

Davis, D.S. (2001) *Genetic Dilemmas, Reproductive Technology, Parental Choices, and Children's Futures*, London: Routledge.

Davis, D.S. and Ponsaran, R. (2008) 'Attitudes toward genetic testing and community representation among self-identified racial and ethnic groups', paper presented at Translating "ELSI": The Ethical, Legal, and Social Implications of Genomics, Case Western Reserve University, Cleveland, OH, May 2008.

Davison, C. (1997) 'Everyday ideas of inheritance and health in Britain: implications for predictive genetic testing', in A. Clarke and E. Parsons (eds) *Culture, Kinship and Genes: Towards Cross-Cultural Genetics*, New York: St. Martin's Press, Inc.

Davison, C., Macintyre, S. and Smith, G.D. (1994) 'The potential social impact of predictive genetic testing for susceptibility to common chronic diseases: a review and proposed research agenda', *Sociology of Health & Illness*, 16: 340–71.

DelVecchio Good, M.J., Brodwin, P., Good, B. and Kleinman, A. (eds) (1994) *Pain as Human Experience: An Anthropological Perspective*, Berkeley: University of California Press.

DelVecchio, Good, M.J., Good, B.J., Schaffer, C. and Lind, S.E. (1990) 'American oncology and the discourse of hope', *Culture, Medicine and Psychiatry*, 14: 59–79.

Denzin, N.K. (1989) *Interpretive Biography*, London: Sage Publications.

Di Prospero, L.S., Seminsky, M., Honeyford, J., Doan, B., Franssen, E., Meschino, W. Chart, P. and Warner, E. (2001) 'Psychosocial issues following a positive result of genetic testing for *BRCA1* and *BRCA2* mutations: findings from a focus group and a needs-assessment survey', *Journal of the Canadian Medical Association*, 164:1005–09.

Dreifus, C. (2008) 'Biologist teaches the nation's judges about genetics', *New York Times*, 1 July, Section F: 2.

Durán, M.A. (2003) *Los Costes Invisibles de la Enfermedad*, Madrid: Fundacióón BBVA.

Durant, J., Hansen, A. and Bauer, M. (1996) 'Public understanding of the new genetics', in T. Marteau and M. Richards (eds) *The Troubled Helix: Social and Psychological Implications of the New Human Genetics*, Cambridge, MA: Cambridge University Press.

Duster, T. (1990) *Backdoor to Eugenics*, New York: Routledge.

Early, E. (1982) 'The logic of well being: therapeutic narratives in Cairo', *Social Science and Medicine*, 16: 1491–97.

Edwards, A., Gray, J., Clarke, A., Dundon, J., Elwyn, G., Gaff, C., Hood, K., Iredale, R., Sivell, S., Shaw, C. and Thornton, H. (2008) 'Interventions to improve risk communication in clinical genetics: systematic review', *Patient Education and Counseling*, 71: 4–25.

Edwards, J., Franklin, S., Hirsch, E., Price, F. and Strathern, M. (1999) *Technologies of Procreation: Kinship in the Age of Assisted Reproduction*, 2nd edn, London: Routledge.

Emery, J. (2001) 'Is informed choice in genetic testing a different breed of informed decision-making? a discussion paper', *Health Expectations*, 4: 81–86.

Emery, J., Watson, E., Rose, P. and Andermann, A. (1999) 'A systematic review of the literature exploring the role of primary care in genetic services', *Family Practice*, 16: 426–45.

Eng-King, T. and Jankovic, J. (2006) 'Genetic testing in Parkinson's disease: promises and pitfalls', *Archives of Neurology*, 63: 1232–37.

Etchegary, H. (2006) 'Genetic testing for Huntington's disease: how is the decision taken?', *Genetic Testing*, 10: 60–67.

Etchegary, H. and Fowler, K. (2008) '"They had the right to know:" genetic risk and perception of responsibility', *Psychology and Health*, 23: 707–27.

Evers-Kiebooms, G., Welkenhuysen, M., Claes, E., Decruyenaere, M. and Denaye, L. (2000) 'The psychological complexity of predictive testing for late onset neurological diseases and hereditary cancers: implications for multidisciplinary counseling and for genetic education', *Social Science and Medicine*, 51: 831–41.

Ezzy, D. (2000) 'Illness narratives: time, hope and HIV', *Social Science and Medicine*, 50: 605–17.

Featherstone, K., Atkinson, P., Bharadwaj, A. and Clarke, A. (2005) *Risky Relations: Family, Kinship, and the New Genetics*, Oxford: Berg Publishers.

Fife, B. L. and Wright, E. R. (2000) 'The dimensionality of stigma: a comparison of its impact on the self of persons with HIV/AIDS and cancer', *Journal of Health and Social Behavior*, 41: 50–67.

Finkler, K. (2000) *Experiencing the New Genetics: Family and Kinship on the Medical Frontier*, Philadelphia: University of Pennsylvania Press.

—— (2005) 'Family, kinship, memory and temporality in the age of the new genetics', *Social Science and Medicine*, 61: 1059–71.

Forrest, K.K., Simpson, S.A., Wilson, B.J., van Teijlingen, E.R., McKee, L., Haites, N. and Matthews, E. (2003) 'To tell or not to tell: barriers and facilitators in family communication about genetic risk', *Clinical Genetics*, 64: 315–26.

Franklin, S. (1997) *Embodied Progress: A Cultural Account of Assisted Reproduction*, London: Routledge.

—— (2007) *Dolly Mixtures: The Remaking of Genealogy*, Chapel Hill, NC: Duke University Press.

Franklin, S., Lury, C. and Stacey, J. (2000) *Global Nature, Global Culture*, London: Sage Publications.

Freedman, A.N., Wideroff, L., Olson, L., Davis, W., Klabunde, C., Srinath, K.P., Reeve, B.B., Croyle R.T. and Ballard-Barbash, R. (2003) 'U.S. physicians' attitudes toward genetic testing for cancer susceptibility', *American Journal of Medical Genetics*, 120A: 63–71.

Garro, L. (1992) 'Chronic illness and the construction of narratives', in M.J. DelVecchio Good, P.E. Brodwin, B.J. Good and A. Kleinman (eds) *Pain as Human Experience*, Berkeley: University of California Press.

Garro, L.C. and Mattingly, C. (2000) 'Narrative as construct and construction', in C. Mattingly and L.C. Garro (eds) *Narrative and the Cultural Construction of Illness and Healing*, Berkeley and Los Angeles: University of California Press.

Gasser, T., Bressman, S., Durr, A., Higgins, J., Klockgether, T. and Myers, R.H. (2003) 'Molecular diagnosis of inherited movement disorders: movement disorders task force on molecular diagnosis', *Movement Disorders*, 18: 3–18.

Gessen, M. (2008) *Blood Matters: From Inherited Illness to Designer Babies, How the World and I Found Ourselves in the Future of the Gene*, Orlando, FL: Houghton Mifflin Harcourt Publishing Company.

Gibbon, S. and Novas, C. (2008a) 'Introduction: biosocialities, genetics and the social sciences', in S. Gibbon and C. Novas (eds) *Biosocialities, Genetics and the Social Sciences*, London: Routledge.

—— (2008b) (eds) *Biosocialities, Genetics and the Social Sciences*, London: Routledge.

Glaser, B.G. and Strauss, A.L. (1967) *The Discovery of Grounded Theory: Strategies for Qualitative Research*, Chicago: Adeline Publishing Company.

Goffman, E. (1963) *Stigma: Notes on the Management of Spoiled Identity*, New York: Simon and Schuster.

Goldstein, D.B. (2009) 'Common genetic variation and human traits', *The New England Journal of Medicine*, 360: 1696–98.

Good, B.J. and DelVecchio Good, M.J. (1994) 'In the subjunctive mode: epilepsy narratives in turkey', *Social Science and Medicine*, 38: 835–42.

Green, M.J. and Botkin, J.R. (2003) '"Genetic exceptionalism" in medicine: clarifying the differences between genetic and nongenetic tests', *Annals of Internal Medicine*, 138: 571–75.

Green, M.J., Hewison, J., Bekker, H.L., Bryant, L.D. and Cuckle, H.S. (2004) 'Psychosocial aspects of genetic screening of pregnant women and newborns: a systematic review', *Health Technology Assessment*, 8: 1–124.

Grimen, H. (2008) 'Power, trust, and risk: some reflections on an absent issue', *Medical Anthropology Quarterly*, 23: 16–33.

Groopman, J. (2007) *How Doctors Think*, New York: Houghton Mifflin.

Guttmacher, A. and Collins, F. (2002) 'Genomic medicine: a primer', *The New England Journal of Medicine*, 347: 1512–20.

Hahn, R. and Kleinman, A. (1983) 'Biomedical practice and anthropological theory', *Annual Review of Anthropology*, 12: 305–33.

Hall, M.A., Dugan, E. and Mishra, A.K. (2001) 'Trust in physicians and medical institutions: what is it, can it be measured and does it matter?', *The Milbank Quarterly*, 79: 613–39.

Hallowell, N. (1999) 'Doing the right thing: genetic risk and responsibility', *Sociology of Health and Illness*, 21: 597–621.

Hallowell, N., Foster, C., Eeles, R., Arden-Jones, A., Murday, V. and Watson, M. (2003) 'Balancing autonomy and responsibility: the ethics of generating and disclosing genetic information', *Journal of Medical Ethics*, 29: 74–83.

Hardy, J. and Singleton, A. (2009) 'Genomewide association studies and human disease', *The New England Journal of Medicine*, 360: 1759–68.

Heath, D. (1998) 'Locating genetic knowledge: picturing Marfan syndrome and its traveling constituencies', *Science, Technology, & Human Values*, 23: 71–97.

Helman, C.G. (1985) 'Disease and pseudo-disease: a case history of pseudo- angina', in R.A. Hahn and A.D. Gaines (eds) *Physicians of Western Medicine: Anthropological Approaches to Theory and Practice*, Dordrect: D. Reidel Publishing.

Hess, P., Preloran, H.M. and Browner, C.H. (2009) 'Diagnostic genetic testing for a fatal illness: the experience of patients with movement disorders', *New Genetics and Society*, 28: 3–18.

Hoop, J.G., Cook, E.H. Jr., Dinwiddie, S.H. and Gershon, E.S. (2006) 'Neurogenetic, behavior, and neurodegenerative disorders', in N.F. Sharpe and R.F. Carter (eds) *Genetic Testing: Care, Consent, and Liability*, Hoboken, NJ: John Wiley & Sons, Inc.

Hoop, J.G., Roberts, L.W., Green Hammond, K.A. and Cox, N.J. (2008) 'Psychiatrists' attitudes regarding genetic testing and patient safeguards: a preliminary study', *Genetic Testing*, 12: 245–52.

Kane, R.L., Priester, R. and Totten, A.M. (2005) *Meeting the Challenge of Chronic Illness*, Baltimore: The Johns Hopkins University Press.

Katz, J. (1984) *The Silent World of Doctor and Patient*, New York: The Free Press.

Kaufman, S. (1988) 'Illness, biography, and the interpretation of self following a stroke', *Journal of Aging Studies*, 2: 217–27.

Kazak, A.E., Segal-Andrews, A.M. and Johnson, K. (1995) 'Pediatric psychology research and practice: a family/systems approach', in M.C. Roberts (ed.) *Handbook of Pediatric Psychology*, 2nd edn, New York: The Guilford Press.

Kleinman, A.M. (1980) *Patients and Healers in the Context of Culture: An Exploration of the Borderland between Anthropology, Medicine, and Psychiatry*, Berkeley: University of California Press.

—— (1988) *The Illness Narratives: Suffering, Healing, and the Human Condition*, New York: Basic Books.

Knoppers, B.M. and Chadwick, R. (2005) 'Human genetic research: emerging trends in ethics', *Nature Reviews/Genetics*, 6: 75–79.

Konrad, M. (2003) 'Predictive genetic testing and the making of the pre-symptomatic person: prognostic moralities amongst Huntington's affected families', *Anthropology and Medicine*, 10: 23–48.

—— (2005) *Narrating the New Predictive Genetics: Ethics, Ethnography and Science*, Cambridge: Cambridge University Press.

Lanie, A.D., Jayaratne, T.E., Sheldon, J.P., Kardia, S.L.R., Anderson, E.S., Feldbaum, M. and Petty, E.M. (2004) 'Exploring the public understanding of basic genetic concepts', *Journal of Genetic Counseling*, 13: 305–20.

Layne, L.L. (1996) '"How's the baby doing?" Struggling with narratives of progress in a neonatal intensive care unit', *Medical Anthropology Quarterly*, 10: 624–56.

Lazarus, E. (1988) 'Theoretical considerations in the study of the doctor-patient relationship: implications of a perinatal study', *Medical Anthropology Quarterly*, 2: 34–58.

Lerman, C., Croyle, R.T., Tercyak, K.P. and Hamann, H. (2002) 'Genetic testing: psychological aspects and implications', *Journal of Counseling and Clinical Psychology*, 70: 784–97.

Lippman, A. (1991) 'Prenatal genetic testing and screening: constructing needs and reinforcing inequalities', *American Journal of Law and Medicine*, 17: 15–50.

Lock, M. (1995) *Encounters with Aging: Mythologies of Menopause in Japan and North America*, Berkeley: University of California Press.

—— (2008) 'Biosociality and susceptibility genes: a cautionary tale', in S. Gibbon and C. Novas (eds) *Biosocialities, Genetics and the Social Sciences*, London: Routledge, pp. 56–78.

Lock, M., Young, A. and Cambrosio, A. (eds) (2000) *Living and Working with the New Medical Technologies*, Cambridge: Cambridge University Press.

Lock, M., Freeman, J., Chilibeck, G., Beveridge, B. and Padolsky, M. (2007) 'Susceptibility genes and the question of embodied identity', *Medical Anthropology Quarterly*, 21: 256–76.

McKhann, G. (2002) 'Neurology: then, now, and in the future,' *Archives of Neurology*, 59: 1369–73.

Macur, J. (2008) 'Born to run? Little ones get test for sports gene', *New York Times*, 30 Nov., Section A: 1 and 21.

Madigan, J. (1996) 'Living with the threat of Huntington's disease', in T. Marteau and M. Richards (eds) *The Troubled Helix: Social and Psychological Implications of the New Human Genetics*, Cambridge: Cambridge University Press.

Marteau, T. and Richards, M. (eds) (1996) *The Troubled Helix: Social and Psychological Implications of the New Human Genetics*, Cambridge: Cambridge University Press.

Marteau, T.M. and Weinman, J. (2006) 'Self-regulation and the behavioural response to DNA risk information: a theoretical analysis and framework for future research', *Social Science and Medicine*, 62: 1360–68.

Mathews, H.F., Lannin, D.R. and Mitchell, J.P. (1994) 'Coming to terms with advanced breast cancer: black women's narratives from eastern North Carolina', *Social Science and Medicine*, 38: 789–800.

Mattingly, C. (1998) *Healing Dramas and Clinical Plots: The Narrative Structure of Experience*, Cambridge: Cambridge University Press.

—— (n.d.) *The Paradox of Hope*, unpublished manuscript in author's files.

Mattingly, C. and Garro, L.C. (1994) 'Introduction: narrative representations of illness and healing', *Social Science and Medicine*, 38: 771–74.

Mechanic, D. (1996) 'Changing medical organization and the erosion of trust,' *The Milbank Quarterly*, 74: 171–89.

Meiser, B. and Dunn, S. (2000) 'Psychological impact of genetic testing for Huntington's disease: an update of the literature', *Journal of Neurology, Neurosurgery, & Psychiatry*, 69: 574–78.

Meiser, B., Mitchell, P.B., McGirr, H., Van Herten, M. and Schofield, P.R. (2005) 'Implications of genetic risk information in families with a high density of bipolar disorder: an exploratory study', *Social Science and Medicine*, 60: 109–18.

Montgomery, K. (2006) *How Doctors Think: Clinical Judgment and the Practice of Medicine*, New York: Oxford University Press.

Murphy, S.L. and Holmes, J.G. (1997) 'A leap of faith? Positive illusions in romantic relationships', *Personality and Social Psychology Bulletin*, 23: 586–604.

Norrgard, K. (2008) 'Ethics of genetic testing: medical insurance and discrimination', *Nature Education*, 1: 1.

Norusis, M. (2008) SPSS 16.0 *Advanced Statistical Procedures Companion*, Upper Saddle River, NJ: Prentice-Hall, Inc.

Novas, C. and Rose, N. (2000) 'Genetic risk and the birth of the somatic individual', *Economy and Society*, 29: 485–513.

Oksenberg, J.R. (2006) 'Genes, genomes, and neurological disease,' *Future Medicine*, 1: 121–22.

Ong, A. and Collier, S.J. (eds) (2005) *Global Assemblages: Technology, Politics and Ethics as Anthropological Problem*, Malden, MA: Blackwell Publishing.

Parsons, E. and Atkinson. P. (1992) 'Lay construction of genetic risk', *Sociology of Health & Illness*, 14: 437–55.

Patterson, J.M. and Garwick, A.W. (1994) 'The impact of chronic illness on families: a family systems perspective', *Annals of Behavioral Medicine*, 16: 131–42.

Patton, M.Q. (2002) *Qualitative Evaluation and Research Methods*, Newbury Park: Sage Publications.

Paulson, H.L. (2002) 'Diagnostic testing in neurogenetics: principles, limitations, and ethical considerations', *Neurology Clinics*, 20: 627–43.

Peters, J.A., Djurdjinovic, L. and Baker, D. (1999) 'The genetic self: the human genome project, genetic counseling and family therapy', *Families, Systems & Health*, 17: 5–25.

Peterson, S.K. (2005) 'The role of the family in genetic testing: theoretical perspectives, current knowledge, and future directions,' *Health Education & Behavior*, 32: 627–39.

Pinsky, L., Pagon, R. and Burke, W. (2001) 'Genetics through a primary care lens,' *Western Journal of Medicine*, 175: 47–50.

Power, P.W. and Dell Orto, A.E. (2004) *Families Living with Chronic Illness and Disability: Interventions, Challenges, and Opportunities*, New York: Springer Publishing Company.

Preloran, H.M., Browner, C.H. and Lieber, E. (2005) 'Impact of interpreters' approach on Latinas' use of amniocentesis', *Health Education & Behavior*, 32: 599–612.

Quaid, K.A. (1994) 'Presymptomatic testing for Huntington disease,' *American Journal of Medical Genetics*, 49: 354–56.

Rankin, S.H. and Weekes, D.P. (2000) 'Life-span development: a review of theory and practice for families with chronically ill members,' *Scholarly Inquiry for Nursing Practice: An International Journal*, 14: 355–73.

Rapp, R. (1998) 'Refusing prenatal diagnosis: the meanings of bioscience in a multicultural world', *Science, Technology, & Human Values*, 23: 45–70.

—— (2000) *Testing Women, Testing the Fetus: the Social Impact of Amniocentesis in America*, New York: Routledge.

Ready, R.E., Mathews, M., Leserman, A. and Paulsen, J.S. (2008) 'Patient and caregiver quality of life in Huntington's disease', *Movement Disorders*, 23: 721–26.

Reimann, G. and Schütze, F. (1991) '"Trajectory" as a basic theoretical concept for analyzing suffering and disorderly social processes', in D.R. Maines (ed.) *Social Organization and Social Process: Essays in Honor of Anselm Strauss*, New York: A. de Gruyter.

Reissman, C.K. (1993) *Narrative Analysis*, Thousand Oaks: Sage Publications.

Richards, M. (1996) 'Families, kinship, and genetics', in T. Marteau and M. Richards (eds) *The Troubled Helix: Social and Psychological Implications of the New Genetics*, Cambridge: Cambridge University Press.

—— (1997) 'It runs in the family: lay knowledge about inheritance', in A. Clarke and E. Parsons (eds) *Culture, Kinship and Genes: Towards Cross-Cultural Genetics*, New York: St. Martin's Press, Inc.

Robinson, G.E., Fernald, R.D. and Clayton, D.F. (2008) 'Genes and social behavior', *Science*, 222: 896–900.

Rolland, J.S. (1994) *Families, Illness, and Disability: An Integrative Treatment Model*, New York: Basic Books.

Rose, N. (2007) *The Politics of Life Itself: Biomedicine, Power and Subjectivity in the Twenty-First Century*, Princeton, NJ: Princeton University Press.

Ross, C.E., Mirowsky, J. and Goldsteen, K. (1990) 'The impact of the family on health: a decade in review', *Journal of Marriage and the Family*, 52: 1059–78.

Roter, D.L. and Hall, J.A. (1992) *Doctors Talking with Patients/Patients Talking with Doctors: Improving Communication in Medical Visits*, Westport, CT: Auburn House.

Rothman, B.K. (1986) *The Tentative Pregnancy: Prenatal Diagnosis and the Future of Motherhood*, New York: Viking Press.

Rothstein, M. A. (ed.) (1997) *Genetic Secrets: Protecting Privacy and Confidentiality in the Genetic Era*, New Haven, CT: Yale University Press.

Sankar, P., Cho, M.K., Wolpe, P.R. and Schairer, C. (2006) 'What's in a cause? exploring the relationship between genetic etiology and felt stigma', *Genetics in Medicine*, 8: 33–42.

Saris, A. J. (1995) 'Telling stories: life histories, illness narratives and institutional landscapes', *Culture Medicine and Psychiatry*, 19: 39–72.

Schaffer, R., Kuczynski, K. and Skinner, D. (2008) 'Producing genetic knowledge and citizenship through the Internet: mothers, pediatric genetics and cybermedicine', *Sociology of Health and Illness*, 30: 145–59.

Scheer, J. and Luborsky, M. (1991) 'The cultural context of polio biographies', *Orthopedics*, 14: 1173–81.

Seabrook, J. (2001) 'The Tree of Me', *The New Yorker*, 26 Mar., p. 58.

Severson. K. (2007) 'Picky eaters? They get it from you', *New York Times*, 10 Oct., Section F: 1.

Sharpe, N.F. and Carter, R.F. (2006a) 'Genetic counseling and the physician–patient relationship', in N.F. Sharpe and R.F. Carter (eds) *Genetic Testing: Care, Consent, and Liability*, Hoboken, NJ: John Wiley & Sons, Inc.

—— (eds) (2006b) *Genetic Testing: Care, Consent and Liability*, Hoboken, NJ: John Wiley & Sons, Inc.

Siegrist, J. (1999) 'The social construction of health and illness', in G.L. Albrecht, R. Fitzpatrick and S.C. Scrimshaw (eds) *Handbook of Social Studies in Health and Medicine*, London: Sage: 100–14.

Sorenson, J.R., and Botkin, J.R. (2003) 'Genetic testing and the family', *American Journal of Medical Genetics*, 119C: 1–2.

Stets, J.E. (1995) 'Role identities and person identities: gender identity mastery identity, and controlling one's partner', *Sociological Perspectives*, 38: 129–50.

Stets, J.E. and Burke, P.J. (2000) 'Identity theory and social identity theory', *Social Psychology Quarterly*, 63: 224–37.

Strathern, M. (1992) *Reproducing the Future: Essays on Anthropology, Kinship, and the New Reproductive Technologies*, Manchester: Manchester University Press.

Stryker, S. and Burke, P.J. (2000) 'The past, present, and future of identity theory', *Social Psychology Quarterly*, 63: 284–97.

Taussig, K.-S. (2009) *Ordinary Genomes: Science, Citizenship and Genetic Identities*, Durham: Duke University Press.

Taussig, K.-S., Rapp, R. and Heath, D. (2003) 'Flexible eugenics: technologies of the self in the age of genetics', in A. H. Goodman, D. Heath and M.S. Lindee (eds) *Genetic Nature/Culture: Anthropology and Science Beyond the Two-Culture Divide*, Berkeley: University of California Press.

Toombs, S.K. (1990) 'The temporality of illness: four levels of experience', *Theoretical Medicine*, 11: 227–41.

Turner, R. (1978) 'The role and the person', *American Journal of Sociology*, 84: 1–23.

Van Riper, M. (2005) 'Genetic testing and the family', *Journal of Midwifery & Women's Health*, 50: 227–33.

Van Riper, M. and McKinnon, W.C. (2004) 'Genetic testing for breast and ovarian cancer susceptibility: a family experience', *Journal of Midwifery & Women's Health*, 49: 210–19.

Varmus, H. (2002) 'Getting ready for gene-based medicine', *New England Journal of Medicine*, 347: 1526–27.

Volkow, N. (2009) Interview by Robin Jay, BMC Journal, 17 May. Online. Available HTTP: http://www.bhcjournal.com/default.aspx?articleId = 18781&tabid = 252 (accessed 27 May 2009).

Young, A. (1997) *The Harmony of Illusions: Inventing Post Traumatic Stress Disorder*, Princeton, NJ: Princeton University Press.

Waitzkin, H. (2000) *The Second Sickness: Contradictions of Capitalist Health Care*, New York: Rowman & Littlefield Publishers, Inc.

Wexler, A. (1996) *Mapping Fate: A Memoir of Family, Risk and Genetic Research*, Berkeley: University of California Press.

Wright, S. (1996) 'It's a yo-yo type of existence', in T. Marteau and M. Richards (eds) *The Troubled Helix: Social and Psychological Implications of the New Human Genetics*, Cambridge: Cambridge University Press.

Index

LaVergne, TN USA
29 December 2010
210403LV00002B/17/P